SIDELIGHTS ON
THE ANGLO-SAXON CHURCH

By the same Author

THE PRE-CONQUEST CHURCH
IN ENGLAND

The Last Supper, in St. Augustine's manuscript.
Some of the Apostles also hold up their hands in blessing.

Enlarged from Corpus Christi College MS. 286, fol. 125.

SIDELIGHTS ON
THE ANGLO-SAXON CHURCH

BY

MARGARET DEANESLY, M.A., F.S.A.

PROFESSOR EMERITUS OF HISTORY
IN THE UNIVERSITY OF LONDON

ADAM & CHARLES BLACK
LONDON

FIRST PUBLISHED 1962

A. AND C. BLACK LTD
4, 5 AND 6 SOHO SQUARE LONDON W.1
© 1962 A. AND C. BLACK LTD

PRINTED IN GREAT BRITAIN
BY R. AND R. CLARK LTD. EDINBURGH

PREFACE

IN the course of trying to give an account of the history of the pre-Conquest church in Britain, some subjects struck me as interesting but needing too specialised treatment for a medium sized history of such a subject. The chapters of this book are an attempt to deal with these subjects, the archaeological, literary and administrative border-line of English church history in certain centuries. Though pre-Conquest archdeacons and deans can hardly be called 'border-line'.

For ease of reading, foreign words in this book are not italicised but printed in inverted commas at their first appearance and there-after without any distinction. Anglo-Saxon proper names and other words are spelt in normal characters, without symbols or accents; for Anglo-Saxon proper names I follow Sir Frank Stenton's spelling in *Anglo-Saxon England*.

My thanks are due especially to Professor Dorothy Whitelock for permission, with that of Messrs. Eyre and Spottiswoode, to print a long extract from Wulfstan's *Sermo Lupi ad Anglos*, from her *English Historical Documents, c. 500–1042*, pp. 855–859; and to Corpus Christi College, Cambridge, for that to print the frontispiece from their MS. 286.

MARGARET DEANESLY

196 Clarence Gate Gardens,
    London, N.W.1
October, 1960.

v

CONTENTS

Contents

CHAPTER I

EARLY CHRISTIANITY IN BRITAIN

IN tracing the early history of Christianity in Britain, and the relation between the Celtic and early English churches, regard should be had to the cultures or civilisations in which the faith was first spread in this country.

The acceptance of the Christian faith always implied not merely the holding of a particular philosophy, but the living of a particular kind of life in the world: Christianity has always, in fact, had to enhinge, incardinate, itself into the society of the individuals it converted. Christians were commanded by their faith to do certain things and abstain from others, at all costs, and this made them at times a tolerated sect, at times a sect which the state would not tolerate. Some relation between the Christians and the civilisation in which they lived had to be established. Christianity flowered best when it had converted the society in which Christians moved; but inevitably the Christian society so formed was influenced by the background civilisation: one Christian 'culture' was distinguishable from another.

Celtic Christianity of the Latin west, for instance, differed from the Greco-Persian Christianity of Seleukia-Ctesiphon in Mesopotamia, and it differed, to a less extent, from the contemporary Christianity of Rome and Byzantium, the fundamentals, in all cases, being the same. You could not have, you never did have, Christianity in a vacuum.

It is useful then to consider Christian history in terms of cultures, and specially enlightening in the case of Christianity in these islands, where at least two or three Christian cultures were fused together in the making of the pre-conquest English church. There was the old Greco-Roman Christianity of the Mediterranean, brought to Britain, no one knows by whom, in the first place: and, in the long run, by far the most important formative influence. There was the Christianity of the La Tène Celts, formed by that of Roman Gaul, and extending from Brittany to the west of Britain and Ireland. There was the Christianity of the Picts (for the Picts were not, indeed, pure Celts), which at length spread from Iona the Patrician Christianity of Ireland. Augustine brought a sixth century Latin Christianity from Italy, and Theodore a seventh century Byzantine Christianity authorised by the holy see. But of all these Christianities, conditioned by their material and intellectual environment, the old Greco-Roman, Mediterranean Christianity was the most important: it was the Christianity of Constantine and his age and it produced the *formulae* of Nicaea and Chalcedon in answer to the queries of a highly civilised pagan, or newly converted world; and the canons of Nicaea and Chalcedon remained authoritative all through early English church history and, indeed, down to and beyond the Reformation. They are those of the English Book of Common Prayer.

The Greco-Roman world was, of course, pre-Christian, and at the eastern end of the Mediterranean, at the time when the apostles and first Christians tried to plant Christianity in it, it was Greek in thought and language though Roman in government. The small state of Judaea was an island in the widespread Hellenistic culture that survived when the political unity of Alexander's empire had gone.

The apostles and the first Christians lived in a land ruled by Rome, but one where the old Greco-Persian culture, the new form of the Greek language and the Greek cities and villas flourished. They could go wherever the Jewish and Syrian traders went, to Antioch, Edessa and Persia, to Ethiopia, and by means of the Mediterranean trade routes to western Europe. Britain lay at the north-western edge of the empire, a large island, but separated by no unnavigable channel from Gaul, and sometimes reached by ships from the Mediterranean that had rounded the western promontories of Europe. Britain only became a province of the Roman empire when conquered by the Roman general Aulus Plautius in the reign of Claudius, in A.D. 43: but, though then inhabited by various waves of migrating peoples, it had shared a common culture with western Europe long before it became a Roman province. There was no ethnic barrier and, it would seem, no great language barrier, between Britain and Gaul in the first century B.C., or later. What central and western Europe received in the way of invading populations and civilisations came, with a longer or shorter time lag, to Britain. So with Christianity: when it reached Romano-Celtic Gaul, it was carried on, almost as part of a culture, to Romano-Celtic Britain.

The most civilised peoples of Britain and Ireland at the beginning of our era were Celtic: there were Celts also in Gaul, Italy, Bohemia and central Europe, the Balkans and Asia Minor. The Celts in eastern Europe had long been absorbed into the Roman empire, but those in Gaul only from Caesar's conquest of 57 to 51 B.C. The Roman empire had by now received many religions from the east: when it began, in apostolic and sub-apostolic days, to receive Christian missionaries and traders, it was possible that Celtic Gaul and Britain would within a certain lapse of time receive them also.

What sort of a world then was it, where the first conversions to Christianity were made? It was a world, from the Syrian provinces of the empire in the east to those of Iberia and Britain in the west, under central rule. Though there might be a struggle over the imperial succession, yet the machine of government remained, in the main, undisturbed. The emperor maintained order on the frontiers by the army: he governed through the civil service, and he appointed the officers of the provinces into which the empire was divided. Rome was an old empire, and astute at combining central rule under Roman law with a variety of local customs and customary laws in the provinces. She had a posting system with 'public horses' collected at different points along the great roads and communications were good.

But though the cities that covered the empire from east to west were administered by local senates ('ordines'), yet by far the most important part of the machine of government was the civil service, entered by free citizens at the lowest grade, after they had passed through a period of education in the rhetor's school. The rhetors were paid by the state and attendance at their classes was free: but the education given there corresponded more nearly to our university than primary education. Boys or young men attending the school would have been taught reading, writing and much else by the slave pedagogues of their fathers: the rhetors' schools were in direct preparation for entry to the civil service. But the learning here provided reached but a very small class directly. Most men were illiterate.

The relation of the small, educated class in the Roman empire to the main body of citizens is of importance for the light it throws on the relation of the bishops and clergy of the Christian church to the mainly illiterate laity. There was no means of extending knowledge held by the one class to the other, except by the human voice. Writings on papyrus rolls, and much more, on vellum, were prohibitively expensive: even the Roman empire, which paid the salaries of the rhetors, provided no books. The Roman emperors, it is true, corresponded with their military and civil officials by letter: but all officers and civil servants addressed those they commanded by word of mouth. Rhetoric, the name subject of the rhetors' schools, was the art of addressing an audience: not in pompous or florid terms, but clearly and effectively. Some rhetoric manuals included methods of memorising the points of the address, to be delivered, of course, without notes.

The very architecture of the Roman empire, and its town planning, was influenced by the need of providing a primitive loud speaker system: of giving a speaker a good position for addressing an audience. Within the villa, as a separate building in the town, the rectangular 'cella' with its apsidal end reflected the voice of the speaker to his audience, and concentrated its attention upon him: while the characteristic shape of a Roman town equally provided a 'forum' for the magistrate to address the people. The forum was a rectangular space at the town's centre, edged by public buildings or the houses of the local 'ordo', and among the public buildings would be the basilica, a colonnaded building raised on stone steps, from which eminence the speaker addressed the crowd in the forum. In the Christian church, quite inevitably, the spoken word rather than the written word was for the catechumen or the Christian the chief and almost the sole means of instruction. The bishops, as the Christian rhetors, with a small number of priests who helped them teach, were set over against the mass of the laity, who with few exceptions were illiterate.

The bishop's see, in the days before Constantine made Christianity a legal religion, was a unit of people taught: thereafter it became, in Britain as well as on the Continent, a territorial unit. In times of persecution the bishop had celebrated the eucharist in his 'oikia' (house), and the area under his supervision was known as his 'parochia' (parish): it was not till later that the word parish came to mean a sub-division of the episcopal parochia. From the fourth till the eighth century, and later, the word parochia meant 'see'. The practice of setting up bishops' sees in the most important population groups, the urban centres, was followed in Roman Britain, as on the Continent, in the fourth century: and it would seem likely that there, as in Roman Gaul, each 'civitas' had its bishop. We know at least that the council of Arles in 314 was attended by three bishops from Britain, and it is not accidental that they should have attended a council there. Arles was the metropolitan city of the praetorian prefecture of the Gauls, and the prefecture of the Gauls included Britain. The church placed a bishop in each civitas, and, as the secular metropolitan city, Arles was the natural site for a council of bishops mainly from western Europe. Church organisation, in this respect, followed secular.

The church in these oral centuries, then, when the faith was first brought to Britain, lived in an oral world: indeed, it remained an oral world for long enough. The bishop was the Christian rhetor, and he taught catechumens and the faithful, in the main, orally. Only the few bishops wrote treatises: all instructed their people, and it was the chief duty of the presbyters in these early centuries to assist them in this teaching.

As to the word 'bishop', and the nature of his office as they were accepted both by the continental Christians and the Celts: the bishop was the 'overseer' and pastor of his flock, to transmit to them apostolic, authentic, Christianity. In the earliest days of the church, while some apostles were dead and some still lived and perhaps presided over a local church, or the churches they themselves had founded, a word was needed for the successor to an apostle. The word 'apostle' could not, at first, be used of anyone not personally commissioned by our Lord. It was unrepeatable: though St. Paul used it of himself, and it was used of Matthias, chosen by the spirit to fill the place in the Twelve once that of Judas. The church then from day to day expected the coming of the Lord, expected that the Twelve would sit upon twelve thrones, judging the twelve tribes of Israel, when he came: it was unimaginable then that there should not be Twelve Apostles, and Matthias was chosen from those who had accompanied the Lord in his ministry, and knew him. While the church still expected her Lord daily and some apostles still lived, no council or debate was held to decide what the successor of an apostle should be called.

The word adopted, 'episkopos', meaning 'one who looks down upon others, who keeps a watch upon them', was the Greek translation of the Hebrew 'mebaqqer' or 'paqid', a word familiar to the early church at Jerusalem because it was used by unofficial Judaism, the desert sects, for the head of their communities. It occurs in one of the documents of the Qumran sect. Like the Christians themselves, the Qumran community regarded themselves as a 'living temple' of people through whom God would act at the last day, and among whom he would dwell, as in his sanctuary. The Qumran community had a hierarchy of officers, elders, priests and the 'episkopos', who was the shepherd and leader of the presbyters. He managed the affairs of the community, admitted novices, and at the solemn communal meal blessed the bread and wine, in that order. The early church borrowed from unofficial Judaism this word for the Christian leader and used it for him who was to replace one of the Twelve, and hold the highest rank in the Christian polity, above that of the presbyters. He was to carry on the missionary work of an apostle. The word had a pastoral overtone and association: 'ye are now returned unto the shepherd and bishop of your souls', and it is this pastoral overtone which has made the Greek word 'episkopos' so difficult to translate. St. Jerome transliterated it as 'episcopus', and king James's translators again transliterated it in English as 'bishop'.

To us, 'superintendent' and 'overseer' have quite other overtones and associations from 'bishop', but it should be noted that there is nothing indefensible in itself in the translation of the word for the holder of the apostolic office. The word 'speculator', the watcher on the tower for the Roman army, had no pastoral implications, but was itself an honourable word: it occurs twenty times in the Vulgate, and was often used as an honourable term of address to a bishop in the middle ages. Bishop Hæddi was addressed in lines written in Theodore's penitential book as

Te nunc sancte speculator.

Pope Gregory III (d. 740) wrote to Tatwin, archbishop of Canterbury, calling him 'speculator et primas' of the whole island; another pope addressed an archbishop of Canterbury even more honourably as 'archispeculator'.[1]

---

[1] See 'Speculator, superspeculator, superinspector', in *Analecta Bollandiana*, lxxvi (1958), 379-387.

The word 'bishop' then from the beginning had this apostolic significance: but the administrative device of territorial episcopates only came into use later. No assumption of spiritual jurisdiction within a territorial boundary was possible in the age of persecutions: and it was only the convenience of having, within the Roman empire, a bishop for a civitas that led eventually to the definition of a bishop's territory. The Celtic Christians, grouped in tribes and without cities, were no less certain than Gallic and Italian Christians of the need to retain bishops as the sign of the apostolic character of their church. Only bishops could transmit holy orders, with them as on the Continent.

The importance of the bishop, in the centuries when the faith was first brought to Britain, was that he was the guardian of theological truth and the organ of the apostolic tradition. He was the accredited teacher of the Christian faith: early icons and vellum pictures of the bishop always represent him as carrying a large gospel book. The bishop's apostolic teaching had, however, to be given orally, for in these centuries all teaching, secular as well as sacred, was oral. Even the students of the rhetor's school depended on their lecture notes for such texts as might be dictated to them by the rhetor: they had no libraries. The rhetor sat in his chair, while his students stood round him, each writing with his stylus on his wax tablets, or with his reed pen on papyrus sheets, or merely listening: and the rhetor's chair was the sign of his teaching office. Similarly, a bishop's 'cathedra', or chair, came to be the symbol of his office: normally, it was set up for him in the mother church of his city, and sometimes his teaching chair was carried from church to church wherever he intended to teach. The chief church of his city became known as his 'ecclesia cathedralis', the church of his chair: cathedral, in the middle ages, was never used alone, as we use it, for that mother church. The bishop's see ('sedes') was only another word for his chair, and it was, in fact, a unit of teaching within the universal (catholic) church: a unit of Christians taught by the bishop.

The bishop, to his Christian flock, was the guardian and agent of the Christian mysteries: but the external organisation of the church stressed his teaching office rather than his sacramental powers. The symbol of his office was not the altar, but the chair. Christian scriptures, it is true, had existed from the end of the first century, and they were held in the greatest reverence: to hand over Christian books in time of persecution to the imperial officer demanding them was the first 'traditio' or treason. But no canon of scripture existed before the second quarter of the third century A.D., so that the convert could not inform himself on the Christian faith by personal study of a definitely limited number of Christian holy books; nor would he have been able in any case to afford the purchase of such a collection, or even of a single gospel. Books were very expensive: individual churches rather than individual Christians possessed copies of the Christian scriptures, more or less complete. In any case, the teaching of catechumens was oral, and the obligation to teach and authority in teaching lay with the bishop.

As to the form of the church in which the bishop celebrated the eucharist: as long as Christianity was a merely tolerated, or at times actively persecuted, religion (as under Decius, A.D. 249–251, and Diocletian, A.D. 285–313) the only buildings expressly built for Christian worship were in Persia, where the edicts of the Roman emperors did not run. Within the empire, the bishop celebrated in some 'cella' within his house, or at times in the catacombs. But in the reign of Constantine (306–337) the religious situation changed: the emperors Constantine and Licinius met at Milan, 313, and a policy of toleration was formulated. The church could come up out of the catacombs and the liturgy could be celebrated openly, not only in the bishop's house, but in specially built churches, and, that all over the empire.

The Christian eucharist was, in fact, often offered in a rectangular cella, with a semicircular apse. Such a building in the days of Constantine and for some time later was usually orientated to the west, as in St. Peter's at Rome. The celebrating bishop, dressed, not in the short Roman tunic of everyday life, but in the long garment reaching to the feet proper to ceremonial occasions, would stand behind the small, low altar, placed on the chord of the apse. He thus faced east and the assembled congregation: it was only later that chapels were themselves orientated to the east, so that both bishop and congregation might face the unconquered sun, now regarded as symbolic of the risen Christ. If the newly built Christian church were large, it would probably be planned as a basilica, or aisled building, with the roof timbers of the side aisles resting on a row of columns, and with probably the same half dome or apse at one end; such an apse focussed attention on the celebrant and was used in other than

Christian buildings of the period, as indeed in the Mithraic temple in London.

Sometimes, again, these earliest Christian churches in Europe were built square, or centrally planned with a domed roof, like the earlier churches in the east beyond the borders of the Roman empire: there is evidence of such churches in Gaul and Italy, but the foundations of none have as yet been found in Britain. Here, some of the new churches would have been built of wood, or, in remote districts, of wattle, like that used for the primitive church at Glastonbury.

Finally: as to the Christian faith in that early Christendom that was the context of Christianity in Britain: the Roman empire was tolerant of diversity of religions, and yet there was something in the Christian claim to the supremacy of their God that made Christians suspect, even when their numbers were comparatively few. A trader, coming from the east, might offer his goose to Mithra or Isis, in the cosmopolite temple on London docks, down at the Walbrook, or a returning centurion set up a little altar to a nymph goddess up near Hadrian's Wall; even the turbulent and religious Jews had special religious concessions. Christians however were not, before 313, a lawful sect: they made trouble about emperor worship, which was practically an imperial loyalty test, and there were rumours about their secret and therefore, no doubt, peculiar rites. Some emperors took little or no notice of them, but when their numbers grew and they were becoming a large and dissident minority, persecution followed. Before Constantine, their bishops and priests were never allowed to hold property, as the priests of pagan temples were; their legal existence was only that of a kind of gild or burial club.

As to the content of their faith, there was as yet no single authoritative statement, but from very early times the professions of faith made by catechumens before their baptism had assumed a credal form, and an old Roman form of such a profession crystallised in very early times as the Apostles' Creed.

But what had sufficed in the way of credal statement when Christians were a persecuted sect, was found insufficient when the educated Greco-Romans began to copy the imperial example, and become Christians. The civil servants did not remain unaffected by Constantine's example, and they had subtle, trained minds. The illiterate masses, too, who had venerated Mithra or Isis or the great mother, began to pour into the church: and if their pre-Christian

2

apprehension of a possible life beyond the grave was useful as a propaedeutic, their ideas about a multiplicity of gods and half-gods were not.

After all, the Greco-Romans were familiar with Saviour gods before Constantine: both the educated and the masses. This Christos whom Constantine accepted must be a strong god, it was apparent: but to the masses he was the same kind of Saviour god as the eastern gods and goddesses: a sort of half-god, who intervened between the blind fate, the supreme, dim majesty that ruled the world, and the obscure thousands of men who were born without any choice of their own, and struggled along, and were killed in wars, and died by the thousand in plagues, and were not of much account, anyway; for whether they were lucky or unlucky, lived long or died young, death looked over their shoulder and beckoned them away at the end, all of them.

But since the emperor now venerated Christos, and no longer the unconquered sun, his subjects might as well follow his example. Christos was, no doubt, a strong Saviour god.

It was in this kind of an atmosphere that further credal definition of the Christian faith became necessary. It was in Alexandria, the centre of the world's learning, where all the mathematicians and all the strange teachers collected, and all the strange sects flourished, that Arius preached the doctrine that Christos was, not God himself (for no educated man could believe that, however much the Christian bishops said so), but LIKE God; homoiousios, not homousios. The council of Nicaea, 325, was summoned, and rejected Arius' teaching; and the council of Chalcedon, 451, further defined the church's teaching about Christ's person, the relation of his godhead to his manhood. In Britain under the Romans, and in the sub-Roman period, some such formula as the Apostles' Creed would have been used at baptisms. When the council of Arles, 314, was held to defend the faith against the African Donatists, three bishops from Britain attended: Eborius from York, Restitutus from London, and one whose name on the notary's papyrus has not survived: he came from the 'colonia Londinensium', which is now accepted as a misreading for Colchester, in the 'civitas Camulodensium'.[1] The decisions of the council of Nicaea against Arianism were accepted by the church in Britain, though we have no evidence that any

[1] EHR. xlii, 79.

British bishops attended so distant a council. Three more British bishops attended the council of Ariminum in 360, when an attempt was made to modify the Nicene decisions in favour of semi-Arianism; it was defeated.

There is no evidence to show that the faith and order of the church in Britain in the fourth and fifth centuries differed from those of the church in Gaul, her nearest neighbour, or of the church at large.

CHAPTER II

THE CHANGE FROM PAGANISM TO CHRISTIANITY IN BRITAIN: ARCHAEOLOGICAL EVIDENCE

THE written evidence about the beginnings of Christianity in Britain is slight: but there is some archaeological evidence about the transition from paganism to Christianity. In the pre-Constantinian period the Christian mysteries would have been celebrated normally in a bishop's house-church: a multi-cellular church, where two communicating rooms would be used for the faithful and the catechumens, and perhaps with a vestibule or sacristy, as at Lullingstone. No separately built Christian 'church' can be looked for before the general 'Peace of the church' of 313.

Before this period cantonal house-churches probably existed, and they may have continued in use for long after 313. The foundations of some Christian churches may still lie under the buildings of modern English cities and towns, for though Roman towns lay desolate at the end of the fourth century, and even more in the fifth century when the troops that guarded their peace had gone and raids and fire had wasted them, yet the invading Anglo-Saxons often built their own towns close beside them, using old Roman building material. These 'burhs' finally expanded over the original sites, and must often have covered the foundations of house-churches. They may still cover them, or even the foundations of small Christian basilicas, or the post-holes of wooden churches. Where the site of the Roman town is not completely covered by modern buildings, excavation may still uncover some traces of Christian churches, as at Wroxeter, Caerwent, Caistor-by-Norwich and Aldeborough.[1]

Bede mentions the church built on the site of St. Alban's martyrdom, by which king Offa of Mercia knew where to establish his minster in honour of the saint, in 793. Bede also mentions churches in Canterbury which Augustine was given leave to repair and use,

[1] See for all this subject Prof. J. M. C. Toynbee's 'Christianity in Roman Britain', in the *Jour. of the Brit. Archaeol. Association*, 3rd Ser. xvi (1953).

including 'St. Martin's', and the old church within the walls of Canterbury 'recovered' and used by Augustine as the church of his see: Christ Church. It has been suggested that St. Martin's,[1] which was outside the walls of the Roman city, was a cemetery church, like that at Cologne under the church of St. Séverin, which dated from c. A.D. 300.

One object recovered from early Roman Britain is an inscription with the words 'pater noster' in the form of a cryptogram, associated with the Christian symbol, α and ω: there would have been no need for a cryptogram after the Peace of the church. It was found in 1868 on some red wall plaster coming from a Roman house at Cirencester: the, at sight, unintelligible line:

α rotas opera tenet arepo sator ω

Other versions of the formula have been found, one at Dura-Europos, where it must antedate 256, and others at Pompeii, antedating the destruction of the city in the eruption of A.D. 79. It has been suggested that the α and ω in this case may derive, not from the Apocalypse, but from a saying of the Lord himself. The presence of the cryptogram in the house at Cirencester suggests the presence of Christians there in the third or even the second century; that Christianity was relatively strong there later follows from L. Septimius' inscription on the pillar, saying he had had to restore the 'prisca religio'.

After the Peace of the church, special buildings could be erected for the eucharist, the instruction of catechumens, and probably in some cases for baptism. Though in the earliest days baptism in running water was preferred, and continued to be used for many centuries in missions to the pagans, baptism by affusion was now common. The foundations of two small basilicas, probably but not certainly Christian (no Christian emblems have been found in association with them), have been excavated: at Silchester and Caerwent.

It is not accidental that one basilica should have been found at Silchester, for the Roman city (Calleva Atrebatum) was abandoned and not rebuilt: the water supply was apparently insufficient. Thus for centuries the small basilica was not covered with other buildings.

---

[1] Not recently excavated: Roman building material can be seen in the walls of the Saxon church.

Its foundations show that it was only 42 feet long and 33 feet wide: it was orientated to the west, and had a semicircular apse, short transepts, and a narthex or porch. On the chord of the apse was a square of black and white mosaic pavement: patches of cement suggest that a stone altar later replaced the earlier wooden one. There was no stone bench round the apse (synthronos), which suggests that a single priest served the church: a bishop would hardly have been alone when celebrating, though, again, it is not certain that a bishop's few clerks would not have stood through the celebration, like the rest of the faithful. Though the church cannot be claimed as certainly Christian, its general arrangement is similar to that of early churches abroad, and a tile foundation may have supported a laver for baptisms. The mosaics suggest an early fourth century date, and the foundations of pagan temples (also found at Silchester) that pagan rites were there practised as well as Christian ones throughout the fourth century.

In Caerwent, however, on Severn mouth, between the Usk and the Wye, symbols, probably the chi-rho signs, have been found in connexion with the site of a late Roman building. The excavation of Caerwent (Venta Silurum) was begun in 1930, and remains of the forum and basilica, existing already at the end of the first century, were found. By the coin evidence, these buildings continued in use till perhaps the middle of the fifth century, and the basilica or meeting place of the local ordo was finally then destroyed in a conflagration. But over the site of part of the ruined basilica, now represented by a burnt layer six inches deep, was erected a small building, some 21½ feet long and 17 feet wide, with a flattened apse at its eastern end, and a curious wide forecourt or narthex at right angles to, and extending far beyond, the walls of the basilica. This is believed to be a barbarised version of a sub-Roman church, used by the small surviving population of Christian Caerwent: the architectural plan resembles that of churches in sub-Roman Gaul rather than the churches of a conjectural Christian settlement from Ireland.

Caerleon, where the martyrs Aaron and Julius may have suffered, was excavated in 1952, and no Christian remains found. As a city of the legions, this is not surprising.

The most impressive of all the Christian sites excavated in Britain is that of the multi-cellular church in the Roman villa at Lullingstone; impressive not only as an example of a house-church, with

Christian emblems on the wall plaster, but as showing how the educated Roman gentleman, probably a high official, changed his religion from paganism to Christianity. The Mithraic temple recently (1954) discovered on the Walbrook served the needs of the Roman man in the street: the soldier, the trader, the sailor: and shows also the affection of the servant or priest of the temple who cut off the beautiful marble heads of the gods, wrapped them and hid them carefully away, hoping for better times when official bans on pagan temples should be reversed. Lullingstone, however, shows the Roman gentleman relegating the busts of his ancestors to a base-ment room, but not displacing the bowls for votive offerings set up before them. The empire under Constantine I and Constantine II became officially Christian, and Lullingstone reflects this official conversion.

There was, after 313 when Christianity became a 'religio licita', no accepted plan as to how a Christian church should be built. When the architects of Constantine I were bidden to build a church over the burial place, or the martyrium, of St. Peter at Rome, they had no models to go upon, and built a great basilica with a small apse at its west end. The apse was placed immediately behind the focal point of the building, the 'aedicula' or portion of an old cemetery wall with two niches in it, one above the other, which the builders covered with slabs of porphyry. No altar was built: a wooden one must have been set up in some association with the shrine. Similarly, no indications of an altar have as yet been found at Lullingstone.

But though so great a church was built at an emperor's command for the shrine of the apostle at Rome (and another without the walls for St. Paul), humbler churches had as yet no necessarily accepted plan. They were built that the bishop or priest might offer the Christian eucharist before the faithful and, behind some kind of a screen or in a communicating room, the catechumens; some kind of an altar was needed, for the bread and wine to be consecrated. The tunnels of the catacombs had been used earlier as chapels, or the 'memoriae', the small, open, cemetery chapels of the martyrs; but after 313 the church builders, commissioned to build a Christian church, copied usually the small basilicas used in pagan worship, as in the Walbrook temple. The Christian altar was small, low and square, like a pagan altar. But in Britain it seems likely that most churches remained the small complex of rooms in either the bishop's house in the town, or in the villa of the Roman gentleman in the countryside. Here, at the villa at Lullingstone, a Christian holy place was superimposed on a pagan holy place, and not apparently by accident, for the villa itself was so large, with a complex of quad-rangles and courts, that other rooms could as easily have been selected. There is no evidence as to who celebrated the Christian mysteries in this high official's villa: it may have been a bishop: but by the middle of the fourth century, in view of the increased numbers of converts and the impossibility of the bishop's acting as the only minister of the sacraments in all his churches, a priest had often become the permanent liturgical minister to a separate congregation.

The villa at Lullingstone was built in the first century A.D. on the west bank of the Darenth, which here slopes steeply to the river. By the coin evidence, the villa was occupied in the Flavian and Antonine periods, but abandoned during the years c. 190 to c. 250. After c. 250 it was reconditioned and occupied and a loggia or garden room built on by digging out the sloping hillside. Antiquarians call this the Basement or Deep Room, but it was not a cellar as we understand the term: it had walls plastered and painted with a dado of hanging vines and bunches of grapes. Two male portrait busts, of Greek marble and more than life size, stood with their backs to the wall, with bowls for votive offerings set symmetrically before them. The busts represented distinguished persons wearing the official Roman costume: one of them, it is conjectured, may have been the owner of the villa before its abandonment. The setting up of the busts and offering bowls denotes the attitude, the 'religio' of those who reoccupied the villa: they desired that the spirits of the first owners should be propitiated with offerings and gifts. The new owners of the villa after c. 250 may well have been some new official family: yet they reckoned that the 'manes' of the old occu-piers were in some sense spiritual powers, and to be reckoned with.

The significance attached to the portrait or 'imago' in the cult of the dead was a well-known feature of Roman thought and practice: realistic likenesses of the dead were held to reflect and perpetuate upon earth the souls of those portrayed. Busts of the departed in roundels were often carved on third and fourth century sarcophagi. Such veneration was, to the Roman gentleman, both sincere and official, supplying the background for the veneration of the imago of the living emperor and his 'consecratio' at death.

The myths of paganism, like the representation of passages in the *Aeneid*, were still held by the Roman gentleman suitable motifs for the wall-paintings of courts and banqueting halls, but no offerings were made before them: their representation had nothing to do with religion. At Lullingstone an apsidal room adjacent to the Basement Room had a mosaic floor, and on it Bellerophon killing the Chimaera, the four seasons as beautifully draped women, and a beautiful design of Europa carried away by the bull, Jupiter, in the floor of the apse: the bull is tearing away over a deep blue sea.

Judging by the coin evidence, the villa had a period of intense occupation and activity in the time of Constantine II (337 to 340). Provision was now made to set aside four rooms for Christian worship. A room was built above the Basement Room with beautifully painted plaster walls, and a second room at right angles to this new chapel, and with a door leading to it, was used possibly for the catechumens at the eucharist. On the walls of both rooms were painted large chi-rho monograms, in roundels encircled by wreaths of fruit and flowers: the earliest Christian symbols discovered from the excavation of any Roman building in Britain.

The new Christian chapel was thus a second storey room, some 13 feet by 15 feet. Its existence is known because when it was destroyed by fire in the last decade of the fourth century (the date is shown by coin evidence), the floor gave way and the painted plaster from the walls cracked with the heat and fell into the Basement Room beneath, where some 5,000 pieces remained undisturbed till recently discovered and rearranged. The complete rearrangement at the time of writing is still unpublished, but enough pieces have been fitted together to show that the west wall had a three feet deep dado, painted as a roofed colonnade with seven pillars and five human figures within the columns. Parts of five figures have been recovered: one, a frontal figure standing before a curtain running on a rod behind his head; in Roman funerary art such curtains are frequently shown behind the dead and show that the soul of the departed has gone to dwell in the heavens. Three of the other figures have the arms laterally extended, in the 'orante' position, the attitude of the Christian at prayer. As the floor was destroyed in the fire, and there was no certain indication of its position on the wall, it is impossible to say with certainty whether it stood in the western or eastern part of the room, or whether there was a fixed altar at all. The orante figures on the western wall in any case face east. When the broken wall-plaster from the Basement Room was examined, it was found mixed with chalk rubble and fragments of *opus signinum* and Roman tiles, and fragments of the portrait busts and votive pots were found buried beneath it. The Roman villa owner had not displaced the ancestral portraits when the Christian chapel was built above them: their position was now less honourable.

The chi-rho monograms in this new chapel and the antechamber of the catechumens are of great interest. This shortened form of the Greek word *Christos* had not only come into general use in imperial iconography, but in a simple form is one of the Christian emblems most commonly found on rings, bowls, tiles, etc., in Roman Britain. These large monograms at Lullingstone however are surrounded by wreaths of fruit and flowers, like those hung on the walls of Roman villas at festivals, and it has been suggested by archaeologists that they stand especially for the risen Christ in Italian and Mediterranean iconography. One Italian sarcophagus, for instance, has a series of panels depicting the Lord's passion, with a representation of the two Roman soldiers asleep at the tomb at the centre of the series. In the solitary panel above this scene of the ending of Christ's life, a panel whose subject could only, in logical sequence, be the Resurrection, there is a chi-rho monogram, wreath encircled, as at Lullingstone. As yet neither theologians nor artists held it permissible to represent naturalistically the risen Christ: even Christ on the mount of Transfiguration was represented only by a plain cross in the dome of the great church at Ravenna. Here, the name Christos, shortened into the monogram, was painted to represent the risen Christ himself. This is confirmed by a detail of the monograms in Rome and Ravenna. In the corner beneath the encircling Roman wreath, a bird pecks at the seeds falling from the flowers or fruit: in Lullingstone one such bird has survived. Roman archaeologists see in the bird feeding on the wreath round the risen Christ a symbol of the Christian soul feeding on Christ in the eucharist: and the decoration at Lullingstone would seem to suggest the same theme. The murals of the Lullingstone house-church attest the Christian faith in the Resurrection and union with Christ in the eucharist; round the worshippers the saints pray with lifted hands.

How long the Lullingstone house-church continued in use is not known. The complex of four rooms, chapel, hall of the catechumens, vestibule and (?)sacristy, could be approached by an outside door without going through the villa, and at some time in the fourth century, while the villa was still inhabited, the corridor with access from one room to the villa was blocked by a wall: the complex of rooms became a self-contained unit. It is likely to have continued in use for some time after the villa was raided and deserted.

At most other Roman villas excavators have been less fortunate in finding and putting together pieces of painted wall plaster. At Frampton, Dorset, an apsidal room was found which may have been a Christian chapel: its mosaic floor had the chi-rho monogram on the centre of the chord of the apse. It is possible that some Saxon chapels were built over the ruins of a late Roman house-church, for the perpetuation of a holy place, or only for the sake of the building material. A Roman villa lay beneath the village church of St. Oswald, Widford, Oxfordshire, and a Roman building under the Saxon church of St. Mary, Lyminge, as also under Southwell minster, churches in Essex and Lincolnshire and under All Hallows by the Tower.

Within the walls of Roman London there must have been the house-church or basilica of the bishop: but the ground has been successively so much built over that no identification of a Christian church has been made. But outside the walls, St. Bride's, Fleet Street, was built on the site of a cemetery where Roman and Saxon burials were made successively; Professor W. F. Grimes has shown that there were Roman walls and a tessellated pavement two feet beneath the apse of the Saxon church, but in no relation to it. There was a small Roman house beside the cemetery, and the site of this Roman house, beside a road immediately without a city wall, is suggestive; and though we do not know whether the graves were grouped round a cemetery church, the siting of the cemetery and Roman buildings is comparable to that of the Roman churches at St. Martin's, Canterbury, and St. Séverin's, Cologne.

Again, for the question whether the siting of Roman villa churches and early Anglo-Saxon churches may be connected, the Roman villas at Llantwit Major in Glamorganshire and Whittington Court may have a bearing. At Llantwit Major carefully disposed and orientated graves were found in an abandoned wing of the villa:

and at the Whittington Court villa a large separate room with a decorated corridor connecting it to the house is reminiscent of the Lullingstone house-church. With the coming of the Anglo-Saxon invaders in the fifth century, Christianity in the early invaded areas of the south and east tended to be overlaid, or to persist only in the dwindling enclaves of the Romano-Britons: towards the north and east the eclipse was slower. The village name Papworth in the Fen country is said by place name experts to derive from the 'papa' or village priest whom the invaders found, still tending his flock.

Though remains of Christian churches are thus comparatively few, the presence of Christians in Roman Britain has been attested by the finding of various objects with the chi-rho monogram, the α and ω, or some Christian inscription engraved upon them.

From a tombstone in a Roman cemetery, now in Carlisle Museum, comes a probably Christian inscription to a Greek gentleman: Flavius Antigonus Papias, 'Civis Graecus'. The age given is 'more or less' (plus minus), which occurs elsewhere in Christian inscriptions, and apparently shows a comparative indifference to a Christian's years of earthly life, since he has now passed to what Bede calls 'the heavenly country'.

Chi-rho monograms have also been found on the hexagonal slabs round a well or fountain at Chedworth, and on three of the eight large lead tanks that may possibly have been used for baptisms. One tank from the Roman villa at Icklingham, Suffolk, has a chi-rho on either side and an α and ω on one side, and other tanks have one or both of the α and ω. All have a fourth century context, and it seems probable that all these tanks, whether with emblem or without, were used for baptisms rather than an industrial purpose, like dyeing or steeping. The Christian neophyte could have stood in them while the baptismal water was poured upon him.

Other small objects of Christian significance include seals with the chi-rho monogram (one from Silchester, where was also found a terracotta lamp with cross and the design of Daniel in the lions' den); a bronze medallion with monogram; and certain rings with monogram. Fragments of a glass beaker have the monogram, the (Christian) fish and a palm-branch; eight pewter ingots found in the Thames near Battersea, belonging to Syagrius the pewter smith, have Christian emblems, and a medallion found with them has 'spes in deo'. Rings and tombstones have the inscription: 'vivas in deo', and two sets of christening spoons have 'Aeternus vivas', 'Pappitedo vivas' and 'Pascentia vivas': it would seem that the spoons were presented to the neophyte after his baptism.

Two Christian objects come from Traprain Law, in East Lothian, the capital and perhaps the 'curia' of the Votadini, the pro-Roman and Romanised tribe who for long defended the northern frontier. The objects are a spoon with fish, presumably a christening spoon, and a 'colum' or wine strainer,[1] an object not infrequently found among the belongings of tribes that imported wine from a distance. This one had the chi-rho at its centre and the words 'iesus christus' round the circumference, suggesting its use in connexion with the eucharist. A small flagon again, from the hoard at Traprain Law, has a frieze of four biblical scenes on its body: Moses striking the rock, the Fall, the Betrayal and the Adoration of the Magi, all in the style of sarcophagi of the age of Constantine. Above the frieze, pastoral scenes signified the heavenly country, to which the Christian was journeying; the flagon itself must have been looted from a church or wealthy Christian official.

Some objects again suggest the fourth century willingness of Christians to interpret pagan pictures and emblems allegorically. It was no doubt impracticable for the owner of a Roman villa lately converted to the Christian faith to tear up the beautiful mosaic floors of the most honourable rooms of his villa: such conduct could not be expected. The Lullingstone owner did nothing about Europa, carried away by the bull, Jupiter; the beautiful Vergilian mosaics at Low Ham, Somerset, would not have been destroyed had its owner become a Christian (there is nothing to show whether he was or was not). But the toleration of pagan myths went farther than that: they were accepted as allegories, and their emblems appear sometimes in conjunction with Christian emblems. A shallow bowl from the Isle of Ely has a polygonal flange decorated with the chi-rho and the α and ω, and also with peacocks and peahens, signifying immortality, the owl for Minerva's wisdom (Christian women went on for centuries invoking Minerva when weaving), and the Nereids who, besides being charming figures, might be taken to mean baptismal regeneration. The fourth century Christians accepted what the fifteenth century Italian humanists claimed

[1] For those found on Severn Mouth sites, see *Antiquity*, cxxix (1959).

explicitly, that pagan religion, like that of the Jews, was a preparation for the gospel; a doctrine reprobated by the bishops.

Excavation has discovered many more remains of pagan temples in Britain, built or used in all periods of the Roman occupation, than of Christian churches. Down till 312, of course, pagan worship and priests were part of the texture of Roman society and veneration of the emperor official. A temple often combined this cult with that of Jupiter: and indeed the veneration of Jupiter was not infrequently combined with that of other gods and goddesses, though not with that of the Celtic and rustic mother goddesses and spring goddesses. The Romans were, in general, prepared to accept Celtic gods and goddesses as local and rustic representations of their own pantheon, and the Roman soldier made his offerings to the local deities.

A notable revival of paganism in the Roman empire occurred in the reign of Julian the Apostate (360–363) and was reflected in Britain by the building of the Nodens temple at Lydney on the Bristol Channel: a temple with a hostel and apparatus for the reception of pilgrims. It was accompanied by the restoration of the column to Jupiter at Cirencester: and probably by similar manifestations elsewhere. The Mithraeum at Carrawburgh on Hadrian's Wall had been wrecked in the early decades of the fourth century, probably by the order of a Christian prefect: it seemed, in 360–363, as if its cult might be legal again: but the pagan revival collapsed with the death of the emperor.

The most notable pagan cult site found in Britain was the Mithraic temple on the Walbrook, whose excavation was rendered possible by the destruction of modern buildings in the bombing of 1940. The site, between Cannon Street station and the Bank of England, was excavated in 1954, in preparation for rebuilding, and the foundations of a small basilica, built down on what were the London docks in the second century, were found.

This small temple (not a Mithraeum in the strict sense, but devoted principally to the cult of Mithra) was sited on the edge of marshy, peaty ground on the banks of the little Walbrook: no other buildings stood between it and the stream, where merchant boats from Italy and the east Mediterranean found their moorings. A bollard to which such boats were tied had been found earlier, a little upstream, slightly nearer the Bank of England. The green and boggy river bank here was not built over: the temple stood on the limit of firm ground, and beyond it, inland, was a poor quarter, where no remains of villas, no mosaic floors, have ever been found. The temple was of stone, 60 feet long and 25 broad, with a shallow apsidal end of nearly the same width as the temple: the remains of a tall, square pagan altar were found on the chord of the apse. The temple was orientated to the west, and appears to have been open to the north, for along the external wall, at floor level, were found the bases of pillars: two other rows of pillars ran parallel,˙ dividing the chamber into aisles. In the south western corner of the temple, where the western wall ran straight before turning into the apse, the Romans dug a square well, whose oak lining boards still remain, unrotted by the peaty water. A lead conduit apparently connected the base of the altar with the well, providing for its purification after sacrifice.

On the wall foundation of the northern colonnade was found the severed head of a marble statue, the locks crowned by a Phrygian cap suggestive of representations of Mithra, god of the light in the sky that comes before sunrise, and also a soldier god. The head is beautiful and unmarred; the unbroken nose and other lack of damage suggesting the hiding away of the head to prevent desecration. It is unusual to find a free-standing statue of Mithra, for he was usually represented in a stone relief as slaying the powers of darkness, and with torch-bearers whose upturned and downturned torches stood for night and day. The head may, however, have been part of a wall group representing the same subject, possibly sited at the back of the apse; a smaller, deeply carved wall group was found near the Wal-brook in the 1870's, which strengthens the probability that this head was indeed that of Mithra, and the temple in some sense a Mithraeum. Mithra was the most popular eastern god of the Roman legionary, and there is nothing astonishing in finding a Mithraic temple in London, where there was a considerable fort for a Roman garrison even before the walls were built.

The temple was not, strictly, a Mithraeum, for this demanded a cave, caves or set of cellars for the celebration of the bull-slaying and other rites, such underground caves or chambers commemorating the darkness in which Mithra fought to bring back the light of day. It would, in fact, have been impossible to construct cellars like those of the various Mithraea in Rome, or that on Hadrian's Wall, for here the water level was too near the surface. But beyond this difficulty, it remains that this temple was built on the plan of a small basilica, with no provision for a crowd of devout spectators of the various rites of the cult. Its altar, at the west end, was suitable for the offering of animals, but there was, clearly, too little room between the apse wall and the altar for the slaying of a bull. Offerings were made here to other gods as well as Mithra: the torso of another god was found on the site and indications of offerings to Attys, the Great Mother, and to other eastern gods and goddesses. This riverside temple seems to have been, in fact, a minor Pantheon. It may well have been sited here because foreigners, eastern sailors and merchants, lived near by, down close to the ships: or because the Roman legionaries or other travellers might here make an offering for a safe voyage or a safe return. The inscription on a small altar found in Yorkshire says that it was offered in thankfulness for a safe return from Italy: this Walbrook temple would have been well sited to catch departing or returning travellers.

The temple continued in use certainly into the fourth century. The whole interior, nave and apse, was then refloored at a slightly higher level, and beneath the new altar, set up again on the chord of the apse, was placed a kind of tray covered with the burned bones of animals (not those of bulls), and with a coin of Constantine I, minted in London. Pagan offerings were, of course, lawful for many years after toleration was accorded to the Christians. The continuance of the temple into the fourth century, with its basilican plan and western apse and altar explains the natural effect such buildings would have on the architecture of Christian churches, if such were built *de novo* at this time. Shelter for a congregation was needed and a recess to concentrate attention on the officiant: also privacy, for the Christian rites were for the faithful, not the unbeliever. The basilica with its apse was copied, but the sides of the Christian basilica were both walled, not open on one side, as in the Walbrook temple. An altar was needed, both by pagans and by Christians, and it was placed similarly on the chord of the apse.

The archaeological remains of cult sites and objects in Roman Britain show (as Professor Jocelyn Toynbee has suggested) that the comparatively few evidences of places of Christian worship surviving may be due partly to the inexpertness of early excavators: the importance of pieces of painted wall-plaster was not early recognised, and difficult to deal with in any case. Most Christian churches were house-churches. Paganism survived into the fourth and fifth centuries: the church in Roman Britain had not converted all the pagans when she was involved in the difficulties of raids, flights and pressure from the new, Germanic pagans in the fifth and sixth centuries.

CHAPTER III

BRITTONIC AND EARLY CELTIC CHRISTIANITY
AND THE WELSH SAINTS

BRITTONIC Christianity in the fifth century had been in touch with the church in Gaul, but the two visits of Germanus show that the area of safety was shrinking: his first visit was made to Verulam, his second to a Belgic king in a more western region. Contact with Gaul was maintained in the second half of the fifth century: the British church learned to reckon her Easter date by the Paschal cycle of 84 years,[1] but she heard nothing of the Dionysian cycle of 19 years, adopted in Gaul. In this second half of the fifth century the Saxon occupation of the south east and East Anglia, together with the violence of local bandits, made life in southern Britain very precarious; they occasioned the notable passage of Britons across the Channel, and what amounted to a resettlement of Armorica, which now became Britannia Minor. The movement began before 450, but was greatest from c. 450 to c. 550: not a folk movement, but a transfer of the more Romanised and Christianised class to a country where conditions were less disturbed. The movement of early Breton, Cornish and Welsh saints shows that the sea passage to Brittany was no great deterrent.

Knowledge of the Brittonic saints of Wales and Cornwall is slender, for information from the saints' Lives is limited by the small number of early Lives, and the unreliability of the later ones. Yet it is sometimes supported by other evidence. There are the manuscript genealogies of early kings, in which occur the names of many Brittonic saints; there are place names, and there are a few inscriptions on stones. It is by no accident that the names of the early Welsh saints so often occur in the royal family trees: for, apart from holiness, it is difficult to imagine how any man not thus connected would have had even the slender landed resources needed to support the life of an early 'llan' or minster. Wales was not a desert island

---

[1] Plummer, Bede's *Ec. Hist.*, ii. 350.

ignorant of private or tribal ownership: a hermit might, apparently, settle in a cave and live in a primitive way on fish, eggs or offerings without seeking permission: but a holy man with a group of followers could not just settle on land owned by tribe or individual without permission. In fact, most saints made their first foundation on land belonging to their family.

Some form of the royal genealogies, again, lies behind part of the material which Nennius 'collected together in a heap' in his *Historia Brittonum*. Gildas wrote less of saints than of royal sinners, and the dating of the two parts of the work now known as the *De excidio et conquestu Britanniae* is disputed: but his description of the five named 'tyrants' can be fitted in with the names in the genealogies. There are some entries of kings' and saints' deaths in the so-called *Annales Cambriae* (annals of the Welsh Britons), though the dating of these entries A.D. is still controverted. From such sources a picture of Welsh Christianity and Welsh saints can be inferred: though in nearly all cases dating can be merely conjectural. The works of Bede, and dating by the era of the Incarnation, were not used in Wales, till the Welsh church, under the leadership of Elvodugus, 'that man of God', accepted the Roman Easter. The *Annales Cambriae* dated the acceptance as in 768.

Welsh society in the mid fifth century, even more than in the east of Britain, rested upon the tribal kings. In eastern Britain such chieftains, using sub-Roman names, had more power than the local ordo of the British 'civitates', for the towns themselves had long lain in ruins; yet in the mid fifth century some 'council of Britain' could still send an appeal to Aetius. But in north and central Wales the Roman occupation had been little more than military, and here the holders of military office became without break the founders of tribal dynasties. Gildas (d. 570) speaks of these tribal chieftains as 'tyrants', a word used also by Prosper of Aquitaine, and the Welsh form of 'tyrannus' was implied. The word 'vor-tigern(-os)' might be used as of a Welsh hyper-tyrant, or as a personal name. Gildas alluded to Vortigern as 'a proud tyrant' without using his name. Nennius in the *Historia Brittonum* represented Vortigern not as a pagan but as a kind of barbarous Christian, who had dealings with Germanus on his visit. The *Historia Brittonum*, indeed, purports to contain four extracts from a lost 'book of Germanus', as well as the genealogies of the Welsh and south Scottish kings.

Of two fifth century personages about whom there has been the greatest historical uncertainty, Arthur and Nynia, there is no mention in the genealogies. Arthur was not a king: and Nynia was a cleric from Bernicia, not known to have been related to any tribal king. Like Patrick, he may have been descended from a clerical line, or the decurion of some local ordo.

Most of the Brittonic tribal kingships, in Wales or (modern) Scotland, derived their ancestry from Cunedda, the federate of Rome, or Maximus, the Roman officer who proclaimed himself emperor. Both Cunedda and Maximus are styled Gwledig (Wledig), or ruler, a title implying Roman authority in the sub-Roman age, and given to some of their descendants.

The history of the Brittonic saints, then, can best be understood in conjunction with that of the great tribal kingships, and as part of a civilisation that regarded itself as Roman and Christian. The word 'Welsh' (wealh) means 'Roman', and the names in the royal genealogies have a Roman ancestry: Etern for Aeternus, Urien for Urbigena, Sant for Sanctus, Emrys for Ambrose, Custennin for Constantine, etc.

For Welsh history, there were three centres of surviving Romanitas and Christianity, the two in north Wales resting on military power, that in the south east, west of the Severn mouth and in Glamorgan, resting on the great aggregation of Roman villa estates, as well as on the Roman forts of Caerleon and Caerwent. These estates of south and east Wales appear to have been the focus of Arthur's power, when he led an army to march against the Saxon invaders. In north Wales, power lay with the descendants of Maximus, who made himself emperor, took away the Roman troops to the Continent, and died in 388, and with those of the sons of Cunedda, sent to drive the Irish settlers out of Wales early in the fifth century. In south east Wales a tribal kingship arose in the Archenfield (Herefordshire), whose king Peibio married a grand-daughter of Maximus. Beyond Wales, but connected occasionally with the Welsh dynasties by marriage, were the kings of Damnonia (Devonshire), Corneu (Cornwall), the Gewissi (Wilts and Somerset), and in the north, of Strathclyde (Alclud: Dumbarton). It was the Romano-British Coroticus (Ceredig Wledig), king of Strathclyde, whom Patrick rebuked by letter for raiding his Christian converts: like Patrick himself, he had claimed to be a citizen of the Romans and a Christian, but this evil deed, wrote Patrick, had made him a fellow-citizen of demons.

In Wales itself, the power of the descendants of Maximus was focussed in Caernarvon (Segontium) and Anglesey, which together became Gwynnedd. They had other Welsh lands and their power was great. Many llans in central Wales and the coastal region south of Gwynnedd were founded by the men and women descendants of this line, and the greatest of them, St. Dubricius, was traditionally the pupil of St. Germanus. The name Constantine (Custennin) survived both within and outside the line of Maximus' descendants: the most famous was his son Constantine, who was proclaimed emperor (Wledig) by his troops in 407, and whose tomb long survived in the fort of Segontium by Caernarvon. His son appears to have been that Ambrose Aurelian, Wledig, who was the rival of Vortigern, and whose possessions lay in Glamorgan, Snowdon (Dinas Emrys) and Wiltshire (Amesbury): and his great grandson was St. Dubricius (Dyfrig). Constantine of Damnonia was one of the tyrants upbraided by Gildas, and elsewhere termed St. Constantine, and Constantine the Cornishman; he was the son of Erb, king in the Archenfield, and of Gwyar, the daughter of Amlodd Wledig; he was the first cousin of St. Illtud. Illtud and Dubricius are the greatest names among the early Welsh saints, and both were of the family of Maximus Wledig.

The patron saint of Wales, however, David (Dewi Sant), was of the line of Cunedda. His father was Sant (Sanctus), son of Ceredig founder of Ceredigion, and Cunedda's son, according to the genealogies.

The settlements of the sons (or grandsons) of Cunedda, as evidenced by place names, lay thus in coastal strips, though some with considerable hinterlands. Cunedda's descendants, men and women, founded llans and became the local saints.

First, the north Welsh territories, stretching along the coast of north Wales and far south from the coast, were settled: apparently as an extension of the Cuneddan power from Westmorland and Lancashire into north Wales: they included Rhos, the territory that fell to Einion Yrdd, son of Cunedda, whose grandson held the fort of Dineirth; Rhufoniog, from Rhufon (Romanus), another son; Dogfeiling, from Dogfael, another son; and Edeirnion, to the south, from Edern (Aeternus).

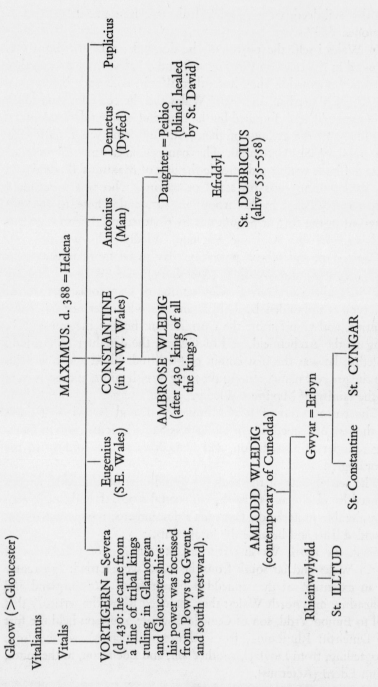

Gleow (>Gloucester)

Vitalianus

Vitalis

VORTIGERN = Severa
(d. 430: he came from
a line of tribal kings
ruling in Glamorgan
and Gloucestershire:
his power was focussed
from Powys to Gwent,
and south westward).

MAXIMUS. d. 388 = Helena

Eugenius
(S.E. Wales)

CONSTANTINE
(in N.W. Wales)

Antonius
(Man)

Demetus
(Dyfed)

Puplicius

AMBROSE WLEDIG
(after 430 'king of all
the kings')

Daughter = Peibio
(blind: healed
by St. David)

Efrddyl

St. DUBRICIUS
(alive 555–558)

AMLODD WLEDIG
(contemporary of Cunedda)

Rhieinwylydd

St. ILLTUD

Gwyar = Erbyn

St. Constantine   St. CYNGAR

THE ANCESTRY OF DUBRICIUS (DYFRIG), ILLTUD AND CYNGAR

CUNEDDA WLEDIG
(king in Manau Gododdin, land of the Votadini)

| Tybion (eldest son, left in Manau Gododdin) | Ysfael (settlement in Man) | Rhufon (Rhufoniog: Romaniaca) | Dunod (Donatus) | CEREDIG WLEDIG (Cardigan) | Afloeg | Einion Yrdd | Dogfael | Edern |

Meirion (Marianus; settled in Wales: Merioneth)

Sant (ravished the nun, Nonnita)

DEWI SANT (St. DAVID of the Mynyws, whence 'Menevia')

Cadwallon

Maelgwn Gwynedd

ANCESTRY OF ST. DAVID

Then, a coastal settlement in Anglesey, called Ysfeilion, from Isfael, another son.

Then, a larger settlement, all round Cardigan Bay, from St. Tudwal's Isles to Cardigan, comprising Afloegion, along the northern coast of the Bay, from Afloeg; Dunoding, at the base of the north Welsh peninsula, from Dunod (Donatus); Merioneth, from Meirion (Marianus), Cunedda's grandson; and Ceredigion, from the Dovey to the Teify, from Ceredig, Cunedda's son.

As to the other tribal kingships: the Roman signal station, Ariconium, would appear to have been late occupied by the Saxons, for the 'Erging', the tribal name of the occupiers, appears to be derived from 'Ariconium'. The name of the earliest Romano-British king of the region appearing in the genealogies, Erb, may also be connected with 'Ariconium': he is called king of Erging and Gwent: the ruler, that is, of the land of the Roman villas.

In Damnonia (Dynfaint: Devon and Cornwall), the fifth and sixth centuries saw the rule of a family of princes, many of whom became saints. Constantine of Cornwall (Custennin Corneu), however (see p. 30), was among the kings most bitterly reproached by Gildas: 'in the habit of a holy abbot' and standing before the altar, he has had two royal youths murdered. There are other references to Constantine as converted to Christianity.

In Kyle, Ayrshire: Coyl Hen, its king, was the great, great grandfather of St. Daniel and St. Asaph; and by the marriage of a great grandson with a daughter of the line of Maximus, of St. Tysilio.

In this disturbed century then, c. 450–c. 550, a half-barbarous, half-heroic Christianity struggled and survived. Christianity was part of the Roman inheritance, which even the violent tribal kings respected and upheld: and the sons and cousins of kings went off and founded in the llans the kind of Christian world, as they conceived it, which barely existed outside. As priests, abbots and bishops they were also the apostles of the pagans, and the pastors of the converted.

The connexion between tribal abbot and tribal king was close, as in Ireland, and this probably explains the existence of claustral bishops living under the monastic rule of an abbot in Wales, as in Ireland. (The seven bishops who attended Augustine's second conference with the Britons could scarcely have been territorial bishops or even abbot-bishops: some or all must have been claustral.) At a time when priests were not ordained under thirty, and bishops much later, perhaps at fifty, it might well happen that an abbot by reason of his birth might succeed to or found a monastery when he was too young to be consecrated bishop. Similarly, he might not have the Latin learning or knowledge of the canons sufficient to warrant episcopal ordination. Ascetic virtue and his birth would yet qualify him to hold the position of abbot.

Nevertheless, recitation of the Latin psalms, reading of the Latin scriptures and use of the Latin rite did secure for the clergy of Wales and Ireland, in these early days, sufficient acquaintance with canonical and other literature for them to know that bishops were necessary officers of the Christian church. Certain senior monks were therefore consecrated bishops: men of sufficient age, ascetic holiness and knowledge of the canons. There is abundant evidence that in Ireland great monasteries promoted more than one of their monks as bishops: it was written of St. Mochta that he had 300 priests and 100 bishops living with him continually: and though this was probably rhetorical exaggeration, there is evidence that Celtic monasteries had often more than one bishop. Dewi and Dyfrig were themselves bishops: but it is likely that there were some claustral bishops in Wales. The old concept of the bishop's office survived: he was a missionary and teacher of the Christian faith, not necessarily a territorial prelate. In both Welsh and Irish saints' lives he is often referred to as writing a gospel book, and represented in sculpture and illumination as carrying one.

The Welsh, British and Cornish clergy, then, kept Christianity and a remnant of learning alive in the west of Britain. The survival in the west, and a temporary defence in the south, was linked with the work of Germanus, for Illtud, the apostle of south Wales, was trained by Germanus, as was Patrick, the apostle of Ireland. The dating of Illtud's life is uncertain: but he had his first monastic school at Inys Pyr (Caldey), and there taught Gildas, son of Cau, a Pictish king in Clydesdale, Paul Aurelian, who worked in Brittany and founded his monastery at Saint-Pol-de-Léon in Finistère, and Samson, who founded the monastic bishopric of Dol. Illtud was famous both as scholar and missionary, and went on from Caldey to found his greater monastery at Llantwit Major (Llanilltud Fawr) in Glamorganshire. In Illtud's life-time Dubricius (Dyfrig) seems to have supervised as bishop many llans or monasteries in south Wales: most of the churches dedicated to him are in the Archenfield, in Hereford-shire. Glamorgan and Severn mouth, land of Roman villas and the most Romanised part of Wales, were the scene of the work of Illtud and Dyfrig: they were the apostles of Welsh as distinguished from the old Brittonic Christianity in Wales: but what they founded was a Gallic Christianity, which they transplanted from Gaul. Both Caerleon, associated with the names of Aaron and Julius, and Caer-went, with its barbarised (?) Christian basilica, are in Glamorgan, and Illtud and Dyfrig worked in a region where Christianity still lingered, precariously.

As to the monastic life of the clergy they trained: the 'familia' of Germanus at Auxerre would have lived communally with their bishop during the years of their training. Priesthood would not have been conferred before the age of thirty, and though some Gallic priests would have been given titles to churches in the city of Auxerre or in the 'rus' of the civitas, and though some deacons might have been sent out to serve oratories and martyria in the rus, the largest group of clergy would always have been the familia living with the bishop. The clergy of St. Martin of Tours were more definitely monastic and ascetic. Thus the tradition of life in an episcopal familia at Auxerre, and of Martinian monasticism, would both have been taken to Wales by Illtud and Dyfrig, and to condi-tions where only monastic, missionary clergy were likely to survive.

The survival, or replanting, of Christianity in north Wales is even more obscure. Here the great names are those of David and Daniel of the Bangors (St. Deiniol). Cunedda and his sons, who brought their followers to north Wales and founded a dynasty of Welsh kings, were little more than Christian barbarians: but Christian personal names appear fairly soon in the genealogies of their descendants. Sanctus, a king of Ceredigion (Cardigan) who ravished the nun Nonnita, had such a name. Their son Dewi, born c. 520, was possibly named David in token of his royal birth and dedication to sing the praises of God: as the son of a nun, he should be offered to God.[1]

He was educated by Paulinus, who had been trained by Illtud, and from his monastery (Mynyw) at St. Davids, he came to rule

---

[1] It cannot be asserted, however, that such scriptural names were given at baptism: they may have been given on the reception of the clerical or monastic tonsure.

other monasteries of the south Welsh peninsula. His own monastery was at the junction of important roads, and he was in touch with Ireland. He was, indeed, associated with the rigorously ascetic movement whose founders in Ireland were St. Finnian of Moville and St. Finnian of Clonard: he and his followers would use no horses for riding or oxen for ploughing, drank only water, and followed a strict rule of fasting and recitation of psalms. Evidence of the episcopal, as well as abbatial, character of his rule is that he took part in two synods, held to establish canons: that of Llandewi-Brefi, in Cardiganshire, and the famous 'synod of victory' at Caerleon. Synodal activity and recognition of canon law and its importance may be associated rather with Gaul than with the Celtic Christianity of Ireland.

Gildas, Teilo, Cadoc, Padarn and Deiniol would seem to have been contemporaries of Dewi. Teilo was born in Penally near Tenby, and was trained by Dyfrig, whom he succeeded as abbot; he himself founded the monastery of Llandaff, which in Norman days became the see of Llandaff. Cadoc, the son of a prince of Dyfed (the south Welsh peninsula), was educated by an Irish recluse; he worked in Brittany, and rebuilt or founded the monastery of Llancarfan (or Nantcarfan), near Llantwit: a famous monastic house. Paul Aurelian, the pupil of Illtud, lived for a time as recluse, and then did apostolic work in south Wales, before he went over to Brittany. Cybi was a Cornishman who came preaching to north Wales, and lived as recluse and monk at Caergybi (Holyhead). Deiniol (Daniel) in the mid sixth century founded the great Bangor in north Wales, Bangor Iscoed, and ruled it as bishop. The monastery was divided into seven septs or subdivisions, and it has been suggested that the seven Welsh bishops who attended Augustine's second conference with the British bishops, held near Chester, were the seven claustral bishops who ruled the seven septs of the great Bangor under Deiniol's successor (see p. 32).

The only one of the Welsh or Brittonic saints whose written work has survived to us is St. Gildas de Ruys, author of the *De excidio et conquestu Britanniae*. This famous abbot, whose llan towards the end of his life was on a high, rocky promontory in Brittany, was the son of the Pictish king Cau and born in the region of Alclud (Dumbarton). He had three brothers, one of whom succeeded king Cau, and the other two led the monastic life in Wales: their names appear in dedications in Radnor and Anglesey. His sister also became a consecrated virgin. But of Gildas himself there is no place name evidence in Wales.

Gildas was born in the year of Mount Badon, and sent by his parents for education to the monastery of Illtud on Caldey. Here, according to his early Breton Vita, he learned the divine scriptures and the liberal arts (the subjects taught in the old rhetors' schools); he certainly read Orosius and learned rhetoric, as it had come to be taught in the sixth century. He even used some of the strange and barbarous-learned terms of the Hisperica Famina in his writings,[1] and he was termed 'Sapiens' in the Welsh and Irish annals. He passed part of his life as an anchorite on a small Welsh river island, and made a long or short visit to Kil-muine (St. Davids), where Finnian of Clonard found him in company with David and Cadoc. He wrote the De excidio in some monastery, 'prevailed upon by the pious entreaties of the brethren', but where is not known. Columbanus when abbot of Luxeuil wrote to pope Gregory I between 595 and 600 and alluded to 'Gildas the writer' as a compiler of canons; this latter suggests that he had attained episcopal rank, though he was not described as bishop in early calendars. He visited Ireland at a king's invitation (the Annales Cambriae say in 565), and the Catalogue of the Saints of Ireland states that the Second Order of Irish saints received the order of their mass from him. His later years were spent at the monastery of Ruys in Brittany which he founded, and the Annales Cambriae give his death as in 570. His life illustrates the transmission of the old Greco-Roman learning to the Celtic church, and the limitations to the learning transmitted: the regard paid to 'the order of the mass', for neither now nor earlier was there anything extempore about the rite; and the way in which the Celtic saints worked at times in Wales, Cornwall or Brittany. Later, they regularly spoke of the life of monastic mission as the 'pilgrim life', but in the fifth and sixth centuries they travelled and worked as widely.

[1] It is doubtful whether the different parts of the De excidio are all by him, or the parts containing Hisperic terms; see Fritz Saxl, Memorial Essays, 1957, p. 54, and P. Grosjean, Remarques sur le De excidio attribué à Gildas, in 'Archivum Latinitatis Medii Aevi', xxv (1955), p. 155.

CHAPTER IV

THE TENTH CENTURY REFORM:
LEARNING AND THE HOMILISTS

Although no great treatise has come down to us as the work of
Dunstan, there is plenty of supporting evidence that he was himself
a very learned man. At no time was he the head of the school in a
monastic house, without administrative cares, and it was those men
who accumulated scholarship and manuscripts over the years and
wrote books. There are casual references and letters, however, showing that Dunstan studied manuscripts even when archbishop, and a
note in one illuminated manuscript claims that it was his work (see
p. 91).

Abbo of Fleury, for instance, wrote to Dunstan, dedicating to
him his own life of St. Edmund, king of East Anglia; he said that
when the life of Edmund was known to few, and had been written
down by none, Dunstan had 'collected' it historically from the
memory of antiquity. He himself had heard Dunstan relate it before
the bishop of Rochester, the abbot of Malmesbury and other of the
brethren: the letter to Dunstan adds, 'even as you ceased not to feed
the brethren with holy words both in Latin and in English'. At
another time abbot Abbo sent Dunstan a poem written with an
elaborate triple acrostic in the Carolingian manner. Later, Wilfricus,
abbot of St. Augustine's, wrote a Life of Dunstan and sent it (between
1000 and 1004) to abbot Abbo to verify.

The reform of English church life and the good will of king
Edgar and his prelates became well known abroad, and surviving
letters attest the hope of princes and abbots that Edgar and Dunstan
might come even to their help in difficulties. A peculiarly Carolingian prelate, writing to Arnulf, count of Flanders, a county (as far
as the letter can be understood) adorned with religion and letters
and the understanding of Greek figures (tropice expressit), and
describing himself as 'the archimandrite of the community of the
confessor bishop' (name obscure), says that he knows that count

Arnulf's munificence is well known in Albion (England); he has therefore sent a messenger through the bishop of Sherborne to ask Arnulf if he will kindly return a certain book of the gospels which two of our clergy, in the old bad days, sold to him. The book was stolen in the Danish raids: please send it back 'for the love of God and his saints' (the phrase in confused and inaccurate Greek). The abbot of Saint-Ouen at Rouen wrote to Edgar, assuring him of the community's prayers and asking his help; so did the community of Sainte-Geneviève at Paris, explaining that they, a house of canons, had been plundered by the Danes and the monastery needed restoration.

Though Dunstan and his Benedictine disciples read the old Latin books and brought about a revival of the old Latin learning, their greatest contribution to English church life in the tenth century was an extended use of English prose writing. Their English treatises were remarkable as literature, but even more remarkable as a means of teaching. They throw valuable light on the impact of church teaching on lay people. It was probably this circumstance that linked the spread of Benedictine monasticism with the pastoral care of lay people. The Benedictines supplied the need for English homilies, English scriptures and the general instruction of the laity in English. Young monks also needed instruction in English, and received it.

Benedictine learning, that is, had no original connexion with vernacular literature, but it was in fact the monks who now wrote good English as well as good Latin, and their writings are held to mark the first great classical period of English prose. They had, by now, a good technique of prose writing, for they were men who had studied the structure of the Latin sentence and the treatises of the old masters of rhetoric; they had also behind them the fine tradition of Anglo-Saxon alliterative verse. And because their novices and some of their monks were simple men, needing instruction, and because monk-bishops wished to instruct lay people outside the cloister, the monks' talents produced a harvest of English homilies, saints' lives and other books. The monks could write Latin: as is shown by the fact that often an English treatise would have as preamble a dedication in Latin, explaining to the critical scholar who might chance to see the book, and question why it should have been written in English, the pastoral needs it was meant to fill.

Among the English homilies, the Blickling Homilies, Wulfstan's homilies and above all those of Ælfric were the most notable. Some, and especially those of Ælfric, were much copied, and though perhaps used first for sermons in a great minster, their substance would become known to rural priests and lay people from their use in bishops' churches where the young clergy were trained; manuscript copies must have been accessible in the book chests of such churches. A high ecclesiastic might have a book of homilies of his own, in his small, precious collection of manuscripts.

The earliest collection of this kind that has come down to us is that of the Blickling Homilies, so called from Blickling Hall in Norfolk where the manuscript was for long preserved. The author is unknown. The nineteen homilies must have been written about 970–980, and though the style is less finished than that of Ælfric, some of the stories and descriptions are lively enough, and written against an Anglo-Saxon background. St. Martin, it is said, was travelling in midwinter with other of the king's thegns, and he saw a naked beggar at the gate of the city; he drew out his knife and cut his cloak, his single garment, in two (he had already given away all his other clothes to the poor); he gave one half of his cloak to the beggar, and the other thegns, his companions, laughed at him. . . . Another sermon had a lively picture of hell, a very cold and dreadful place; St. Paul, mentioned in the sermon, looked to the north and there he saw a rocky, ice-covered cliff towering above the black waters of the sea, where water monsters dwelt and all accursed things. On the edge of the cliff grew trees, their boughs all white with rime and frost, and from the ice-covered boughs he saw hanging many blackened souls, their hands tied together; devils like sea monsters snapped at them like wolves. Then when the boughs broke, the souls that hung from them fell down the rocky cliff to the dark sea, and the monsters seized upon them. . . .

But the Blickling Homilies are much more concerned with pastoral admonition than picturesque detail. The bishop, one passage runs, must constrain the mass priests with love or fear to observe God's law, and the familia (hird) over whom they are set; and the simple men (laity) over whom they ought to be ealdormen. . . . For the bishop is God's vassal and equal in holiness with the apostles and in rank with the prophets. . . . As the noble teacher St. Paul has said: the king and the bishop shall be shepherds of Christian folk and turn them from all unrighteousness. And another passage lays down that the bishop and the mass priest, if they be rightly God's servants (theows: the translation of servi, serfs, slaves), shall serve God's people daily, or at least once a week sing mass for all Christian folk . . . and those that are in heaven shall intercede for those who are engaged in this song. Elsewhere, great personages are specified as bishops, kings, mass priests, high deacons (heahdiaconas), and those of lesser rank, as sub-deacons and monks. The 'high deacons' would seem to be archdeacons, or merely the chief deacons in an episcopal familia (see p. 149).

Other passages are addressed to the lay people, or make clear some church doctrine to them. All Christian men should 'sign their whole bodies with the sign of the cross', seven times a day: first, early in the morning, then about nine o'clock, at noon tide, about three o'clock, then in the evening, then when they go to bed: and the seventh time at dawn. 'And I counsel you, my brothers, that ye give the tenth of your sceattas (Anglo-Saxon coins) to poor men, who before the world have but little', for 'the end of this world is very nigh.' 'The lord Christ dwelt here in this world along with men': 'for the queen of all virgins gave birth to the Creator and Comforter of all people, the Saviour of all the world: the golden-blossom sprang up in this world.' The veneration of relics is taken for granted, and it is told how the footsteps of Christ on the top of the Mount of Olives are today protected by a great church, open and unroofed, so that men may look up into heaven as the apostles did when Christ ascended: and the footsteps are within an enclosure as large as a bushel basket and high as a man's breast: and pilgrims take earth from the footsteps, yet they ever remain plain . . . in the great church there are eight windows and before each a lamp burns all night, 'very light and bright do these lamps shine all night through the windows'.

The reformed Old Minster under Æthelwold was a house of studies, and Ælfric[1] the homilist its most illustrious pupil. There was, from the first, a tradition that the monks should speak Latin, and well understand what was written in Latin. Æthelwold himself translated, c. 960, the Benedictine rule into English, king Edgar inciting him; his version translated according to the sense, and ran

---

[1] See p. 42 for the Old English Benedictine Office, and the relations between Ælfric and Wulfstan, *Anglia*, iii (1960).

smoothly and easily. His young monk pupil (c. 955-?1020) had already had some teaching before he entered the minster: he speaks in one homily of having had as his teacher an old mass priest who had the book of Genesis and was able to understand some Latin; but he did not know the difference between the Old Testament and the New, nor did Ælfric at that time. He was trained in the Benedictine school of Æthelwold for many years, till Æthelwold died in 984, and then under his successor, bishop Ælfheah II. He was already a priest and therefore over thirty when Ælfheah sent him off to the new little minster at Cerne Abbas in 987.

This minster was founded by Æthelmær, the son of ealdorman Æthelweard, and both men were to be Ælfric's patrons and supporters throughout his life. The ealdorman Æthelweard signed himself 'duke of the western provinces': he was the king's representative, that is, in more than a shire: he was responsible for Somerset, Dorset and Devon, and his son Æthelmær is mentioned later as earl of Cornwall and Devon. He endowed the house at Cerne from family lands in these shires. Æthelweard was a great and wealthy personage, and for his day a very learned layman; he was probably the Æthelweard who thought fit to turn a very early version of the Anglo-Saxon Chronicle into curious Latin, and like a few other Wessex thegns of the day, he desired to possess what English works of Ælfric he could. The house at Cerne, that is, was founded by learned laymen in the Alfredian tradition. At some time it had in its possession the beautifully illuminated gospels of the Passion and Resurrection known as the Book of Cerne; this manuscript was written originally at Lichfield and presumably saved from Danish raiders and given to the monks of Cerne.

At Cerne Ælfric taught the young monks monastic virtue, how to speak good Latin, to understand about the computus, and to meditate upon the feasts of the liturgical year; his series of homilies deal both with the feasts of our Lord and those of the saints. His most memorable treatises were written at Cerne, where he had the less administrative work, and where he lived as a monk, like Bede; but in 1005 Æthelmær founded a second minster, at Eynsham, in Oxfordshire, and Ælfric became abbot there till his death. In all his English works, biblical translations, homilies, letters and canons meant to be read in a diocesan synod, Ælfric showed himself a great teacher and a writer of clear, lucid English; his knowledge of Latin syntax and

4

rhetoric lies behind his distinguished English writing. He had left behind the glossarial Latin of the earlier Celtic scholars, and made no attempt to use an artificial style in English.

Ælfric's works[1] included two series of Anglo-Saxon homilies, which he dedicated to Sigeric, archbishop of Canterbury 990–994; a third series of homilies; Lives of the saints in a kind of alliterative, rhythmical prose; an English translation or paraphrase of selected passages of the Heptateuch; a set of canons, and two pastoral letters. He wrote also a Latin grammar and glossary, a Latin commentary and expansion of Bede's *De temporibus* and a Latin *Colloquium* or dialogue between a master and his pupil who desired to have a good Latin vocabulary, so that he might converse in Latin really well: this had an English interlinear translation.

Besides these treatises Ælfric wrote certain other Latin works of importance: a life of St. Æthelwold, described in the preface as by an alumnus of Winchester and dedicated to Coenwulf, bishop of Winchester in 1006; a Latin abridgment of the Benedictine rule, as edited by Æthelwold in the *De Consuetudine Monachorum*: this he wrote specially for the monks of Eynsham; a pastoral letter for Wulfstan II, archbishop of York, 1002–1023, dealing with clerical chastity, the use of the holy oil, etc.; a letter to Sigferth, dealing with the celibacy of the clergy, etc., and a few other pieces.

As to Ælfric's English homilies, his most considerable work: he entitled the first and second series *Catholic Homilies* (*Homiliae Catholicae*) because they were written as 'sermons' for feasts in the church's year which all Christians kept; his third set of homilies on the other hand dealt with saints 'whom monks honour', local and other saints, that is, whose feasts were not prescribed for universal observance. The *Catholic Homilies* were, in fact, selected passages translated from the Christian Fathers, according to the sense, not the letter; the feasts for which they were written included those of apostles and evangelists, Christmas, St. Stephen, 'Shrove Sunday', the Sundays in Lent, Easter, the Ascension, Pentecost, St. John Baptist, the Assumption, St. Michael, All Saints and St. Andrew, together with a few Lives and Passions of other saints; they dealt also with baptism, the housel and true penance.

His sermon for Holy Innocents day illustrates the sympathy of his

---

[1] See *Chapters on Old English Literature*, Wardale, E. E., 1935, 271, and for chronology of works, pp. 215-247 of *The Anglo Saxons*, ed. Clemoes, P., 1959.

mind and the poetic quality of his writing. Christ, he wrote, did not forget these young warriors: he sent them from this life of misery to his eternal kingdom. Happy was the hour of their birth, that for his sake they might die. Blessed was their age, for not yet being able to confess Christ, they yet might suffer for him. They were witnesses to the Saviour, whom as yet they knew not. They were old enough to be slaughtered: yet they died most blessedly unto life. They were torn from their mothers' breasts, but gathered to the breasts of angels and carried away. They are called the flowers of the martyrs: for they sprang up like flowers in the winter cold, and were cut down by the frost of persecution.

The sermon of Ælfric for Septuagesima Sunday begins with a solemn warning, appropriate to the season, but goes on to speak of God's boundless mercy. 'The ending of this gospel (for the day)', he says, 'is surely full of dread: Many are called and few are chosen. . . . Two things there be that we should carefully give heed to: first that none of us be too boldly confident in himself: next, that none of us despair of his neighbour, though he have fallen into sins, for we cannot measure the great mild-heartedness of God. The psalm scop beheld this great mild-heartedness when he cried to God: My helper, of thee I sing, for that thou, God, art my Receiver, my God, and my mercy. . . . He would not call God merciful, but called him mercy itself, saying: My God and my mercy (mild-heartedness). . . . God's mercy steppeth before us, and his mercy followeth us. When we willed not good, God's mercy rode before us, so that we did will good. Now that we will well, God's mercy followeth us, that our will be not in vain.'

The third series of homilies has a preface where Ælfric says he has translated from Latin into English the Passions and Lives venerated by monks, and this at the request of Æthelweard and his son Æthelmær. There is a homily for Ash Wednesday, where he says that throughout the whole world priests bless clean ashes and lay them upon men's heads, and, incidentally in the course of the homily, that Sunday is so joyful a day that 'we eat at the third hour' and 'neither may anyone kneel on Sunday'. For St. George's day he wrote that 'Heretics have written in their books about the holy man called George: we now will tell you that which is true about him' (George suffered in Cappadocia in the Decian persecutions: nothing is said about any dragon). For St. Alban, Ælfric followed Bede, saying that

Alban went with the persecutors dressed in the priest's cloak, hoping to save the priest he had hidden: where Bede spoke of the priest's Gallic, hairy cloak, Ælfric uses the common word for cloak (hakelan), which was also combined with 'mass' for 'chasuble'. (A chasuble was described in English, that is, as a 'mass cloak', mæsse hacele). In a sermon on auguries, Christian people were warned not to inquire of witches: 'Some men are so blinded that they bring their offering to an earth-fast stone and else to trees and to well-springs, even as witches teach'. In another homily there is a reference to keeping vigil by a corpse, with a rebuke for them who 'doltishly jest at dead men's corpses' and 'drink the whole night at a like-wake'. . . . 'No beer is seemly at a wake', but rather, holy prayers are fitting there.

Perhaps the most historically interesting of all the saints' lives is that of St. Swithun, who had been bishop in the Old Minster at Winchester from 852 till his death on July 2, 862. The ASC. says nothing of him: but the years of his episcopate were full of Danish raids, and for Kent and East Anglia the situation was already very bad: in 853 the heathen men for the first time wintered in Sheppey. In 860 'a great pirate host landed and stormed Winchester'. The urgent military dangers perhaps account for the lack of records of bishop Swithun: but he rebuilt his cathedral church of Winchester (see p. 96) and a tradition of holiness seems to have been handed down. It must have underlain the popular acceptance of miracles worked at his intercession nearly a century later. The story is of interest as that of the origin and development of a popular cult; its acceptance and authorisation by the authorities of the reformed Old Minster, which now found itself protected by a new heavenly patron, and for the light casually thrown on the lives and status of those who received miraculous help, or were mentioned in the stories: a crippled thegn, a serf woman, and a canon of the Old Minster ejected by Æthelwold and naturally displeased with him.

Ælfric's account indeed relates the story, not of Swithun's life, but of his miracles and canonisation:

His deeds were not known before God himself manifested them: neither have we found in books how the bishop lived in this life, before he departed to Christ. In the days of the noble king Edgar, Ælfric relates, when by God's grace Christendom was thriving well among the English, God revealed the greatness of St. Swithun by many wonders.

This Swithun was bishop in Winchester, as it were over Hamptun-scire: he was a blessed servant of God. There were eight bishops between him and St. Æthelwold. He was buried at his bishop's stool, to the west of the church, in a stone coffin.

Three years before he was brought into the church out of the stone coffin, St. Swithun appeared to a certain faithful smith in a vision, saying to him: 'Dost thou know the priest called Eadsige, who with other priests was driven out of the old minster, for misconduct?'

The smith answered that he knew him long ago: but he had departed, and the smith knew not his dwelling: to which the holy man answered that he had settled and dwelt in Winchcombe: the smith must tell him that Swithun the bishop has commanded him to go to bishop Æthelwold and bid him open the grave and bring his bones within the church.

And the smith said to him: 'Oh, sir, Eadsige will not believe my words': and was bidden tell Eadsige to go to the grave and lift the ring on the coffin, as a sign: if the ring would not be lifted, then should he in nowise believe the smith's saying. Still the smith hesitated, and three times the saint appeared to him, bidding him go: and finally the smith himself went to the grave and pulled up the ring from the coffin, praying to God to show him the truth: and he drew the iron out of the stone easily.

Then, awestricken, the smith replaced the ring, and it stood so fast, no man could draw it therefrom. And he went thence and met in the market place Eadsige's man, and told him exactly what Swithun had bidden him, and asked him to tell it to Eadsige. The man too hesitated, but finally told him in order what Swithun had enjoined him. But Eadsige at that time would have nothing to do with Æthelwold because of the expulsion, and he would not obey the saint's command, though he was of St. Swithun's kindred. (But in two years, by the grace of God, he retreated to that same monastery and became a monk there till his life's end.)

But there was a certain poor ceorl, dreadfully humpbacked: and to him too Swithun appeared in a dream, bidding him pray at his grave and receive healing. And he arose in the morning and crept to Winchester on two crutches, and kneeled as he was bidden and prayed for healing: and the holy bishop healed him so that no man could see that he had ever been humpbacked. And the monks knew not of the great saint, and thought some other saint had healed him. But the ceorl said Swithun had healed him, as he knew well.

Then another sick man, almost blind and dumb, was brought to the new minster for healing by St. Judoc: but someone told him that it would be better to be taken to the old minster, to Swithun's grave. And his friends watched with him through the night, and at daybreak it seemed to the sick man that the tomb rocked: and he was healed. Eight sick men there were, miraculously healed by God, before Swithun was taken up out of the tomb.

Then king Edgar desired that the holy man should be taken up: and he spoke to the worthy bishop Æthelwold, bidding him translate him with great pomp. And bishop Æthelwold with abbots and monks took up the saint with solemn chanting and bore him into the church, St. Peter's house. 'There he abideth in honour and worketh wonders.'

Then followed the account of how, during five months 'there were few days when there were not healed at least three sick persons'; within ten days, two hundred men were healed: 'the burial ground lay filled with crippled folk, so that people could hardly get into the minster', and they were all miraculously healed.

About the same time, a certain slave woman was caught to be flogged for a slight guilt, and she was kept in custody to be severely beaten for it in the morning. And all the night she lay awake and cried with weeping to St. Swithun, that he would help her, a poor wretch, and with God's might deliver her from the cruel stripes. And at dawn, when the monks began lauds, the fetters fell from her feet, and she ran to the church, to the blessed saint, her hands still bound: and her lord came after her and loosed her hands, and freed her at once for Swithun's honour.

And a certain thegn lay long, crippled by paralysis: and for many years he could not stir from his bed. And he said he would journey to Winchester on a horse litter, and pray to be healed; and as he said this, he was healed: but none the less he went to the saint, walking on his feet, and gave thanks to the saint for his recovery.

And there were many other miracles: and a rich thegn who had travelled to Rome for healing and gained it not, was healed by St. Swithun; and another man, blind and led by a guide for seven years, was deserted by his guide, and prayed to the 'mild bishop, from whom come many miracles through the living God' and was healed, and went blithely home, without any guide: and his kinsmen rejoiced greatly.

Then Æthelwold, the blessed bishop, bade all his monks who dwelt in the minster to go in procession into the church and magnify God for the great saint, as often as any sick man was healed.

Then forthwith they did so, and sang the *Te Deum*, until they all loathed to arise so often, sometimes three and sometimes four times in a night, to sing the *Te Deum*, when they wanted to sleep.

And at last they left off the chanting, because the bishop was busy with the king, and knew not that they had ceased to sing *Te Deum*. But St. Swithun appeared to a certain good man in a vision, and bade him go to the minster and rebuke the monks for their sloth in not singing the hymn. And the man arose and went very quickly to bishop Æthelwold and told him all this: and Æthelwold sent at once from the king's household and bade the monks sing the *Te Deum*, as he had appointed. 'Thenceforth they ever observed this custom, as we ourselves have very often seen, and have not seldom sung this hymn with them.'

Though in the homily on Swithun so many miracles are recorded, as indeed not extraordinary to men who believed with simplicity that the saints were as ready to do kindnesses in heaven as they had been on earth, yet Ælfric as a good pastor inserts a warning about miracles:

Nevertheless it is to wit, that we must not pray to God's saints as to God himself, because he alone is God and above all things, but we should truly pray the saints to intercede for us with the all-ruling God who is their lord, that he may help us.

Of all Ælfric's homilies, that on the sacrifice on Easter Day, or 'the Paschal Lamb', has given rise to most controversy. It was written to explain to simple and unlearned people how 'the holy housel' to which they were going could be, through the priest's hallowing, the body and blood of Christ. Ælfric was writing indeed long before the treatises and definitions of medieval scholars had been thought out; when the mind of the church, moving against a background of Platonic thought, accepted but had not yet explained the mode of Christ's presence. Ælfric lived long before, in the west, the metaphysical explanation had been arrived at, that a change of 'substance' in the consecrated elements was a material change. Ælfric uses the term 'figure', but with the contemporary scriptural implication. The mind of God being ever immutable, and ruling human history, Christ was present 'in figure' in the Old Testament as in the New: Jacob and Joseph were Christ 'in figure': as the bread in the eucharist.

Ælfric had behind him, and had well digested, the Christian Fathers' and especially Gregory's thought that, in the immutable mind and will of God, and his foreknowledge of Christ in the ages before his birth, certain people and things in the scriptures prefigured Christ; and this in much more than the sense of casual resemblance or the similarity of the events of their lives, e.g. 'They drank of the spiritual rock that followed them, and that rock was Christ'; which is a passage quoted in the Paschal sermon. In a sense it could be said that Moses and Joseph and David, in the foreknowledge of God, were Christ: or, in Ælfric's phrase, they 'betokened Christ'.

Ælfric's favourite English word for the explanation of a mystery is the Old English verb 'getacnian', the translation of the Latin word 'significare', as 'tacen', token, is the word for a sign: Adam, said Ælfric, betokened our Saviour Christ: the lamb betokened was offered at Easter tide. When he says that the consecrated bread 'betokens Christ', the Latin word in his mind is 'Christum significat': the bread seen by all men is the sign of Christ's presence. It was very long before the terms 'substance and accidence' would come into use: Ælfric was explaining to simple people that here was Christ.

Those who in the sixteenth century took this Easter sermon of Ælfric as evidence that he shared their views about the sacrament, denying any change of substance, ignored the chasm in thought between their age and Ælfric's and interpreted it in the light of Protestant theology; of doctors who regarded the eucharist merely as a commemoration, and revered the presence of Christ not in the sacrament but in the exposition of the divine word.

Perhaps more important for the understanding of this Easter homily than Ælfric's pre-dating of the medieval philosophies about the sacramental change is his pre-dating of the terms literal, typical, allegorical, as applied to the interpretation of scripture. It is true that Gregory the Great had emphasised in his writings the manifold possible interpretations of scripture, and particularly the allegorical interpretations of passages in the Old Testament. But the doctrine of a fourfold interpretation, and its terms, were not yet cut and dried: they did not yet come to Ælfric's mind: and when they have been sometimes used to translate Anglo-Saxon expressions used by Ælfric, they imply something more than was in his mind, or something less. 'Typically' as contrasted with 'literally' are inadequate translations,[1] implying the philosophies of later centuries.

The best way, that is, that Ælfric can explain the holy housel to the simple, is to repeat Christ's words of institution and say that the holy housel 'betokens Christ'; signifies Christ. The relevant passages in the long homily run:

> Men most beloved,[2] it has frequently been related to you concerning our Saviour's (Hælendes) resurrection, how he on this present day, after his passion, arose mightily from death. Now will we open to you, through God's grace, concerning THE HOLY HOUSEL, to which ye now shall go, and direct your understanding about that mystery both according to the Old Testament and according to the New, lest any doubt afflict you concerning the living feast.

(Passage about the spiritual significance of the innocent lamb slaughtered at the Passover, in reference to which God's servants (theowas) sing at every mass 'Agnus dei, qui tollis peccata mundi, etc.')

> The people of Israel ate the flesh of the lamb at their Eastertide, when they were delivered, and we now spiritually partake of Christ's body and drink his blood, when we with true belief partake of the holy housel . . . we Christian men hold Christ's resurrection as our Eastertide, during these seven days . . . and we shall be purified by this going to the holy housel (husel-gangen), as Christ himself said in his gospel: 'Soothly, soothly I say to you, ye have no life in you, except ye eat my flesh and drink my blood. He that eateth my flesh and drinketh my blood, he dwelleth in me, and I in him, and he shall have eternal life, and I will raise him up at the last day. I am the living bread (liflica hlaf) that came down from heaven. Not in the way that your forefathers ate the heavenly meat in the wilderness and afterwards died: he that

---

[1] See Thorpe, B., *The homilies of the Anglo-Saxon church*, ii, 1846, 269.
[2] *Ib.* ii, 263.

eateth this bread shall live to eternity.' He hallowed this bread before his passion and dealt it out to his disciples, saying thus: 'Eat this bread, it is my body, and do this in my remembrance.' Afterwards he blessed wine in a cup (calice) and said: 'Drink ye all of this: this is my blood, which shall be shed for many in forgiveness of sin.' The apostles did as Christ commanded, in that they hallowed bread and wine for the housel in his remembrance. Even so their successors (æftergencgan, aftercomers) and all priests, at Christ's behest, hallow bread and wine to the housel in his name, with the apostolic blessing.

Now certain men have often inquired and yet frequently do inquire, how this bread, that is prepared from corn and baked through the heat of fire, may be changed to Christ's body? or the wine, that is pressed from many berries, may be changed through any blessing to the Lord's blood?

Now say we to such men, that some things are said of Christ through betokening, and some through the known thing. It is a true and known thing that Christ was born of a maiden, and of his own will suffered death and was buried: and on this day he arose from the dead. He is called bread through betokening, as also lamb and lion and whatever else. . . . Why then is the holy housel called Christ's body or his blood, if it is not soothly (after its true nature: æfter sothum gecynde) what it is called? Soothly, the bread and wine that are hallowed through the mass of the priests appear one thing to human perception and another thing to believing minds within. Without, they appear bread and wine, both in appearance and taste: and yet they are soothly, after the hallowing, Christ's body and blood through a ghostly mystery.

(Ælfric continues in illustration to point out that when a heathen child is baptised its outward appearance is not changed, though it is changed within; and so the holy font-water, that is called life's well-spring, looks like any other water. . . . Great is the difference between the unseeable might of the holy housel and the seeable appearance in its own nature. By its nature, it is corruptible bread, and by the power of the divine (God-natural) word, it is truly Christ's body and his blood: not bodily but spiritually.)

This mystery is pledge and symbol: Christ's body is truth. This pledge we hold mysteriously until we come to the truth, and then will this pledge be ended. . . . Ye are not to inquire how it is done but to hold in your belief that it is so done.

This tide is in the Hebrew PASCHA, that is in Latin, 'Transitus' and in English 'Passover'. . . . Our Lord passed at this time, as the gospeller John saith, from this middle world to his heavenly Father. We should follow our Head and pass from the devil to Christ, from this unsteady world to his steadfast kingdom . . . and after this transitory life to life everlasting, and after our resurrection to our Saviour Christ . . . to the world of all worlds. Amen.[1]

Ælfric's homilies afford evidence of his skill as a translator, for they contain English renderings of many passages from scripture, the gospels as well as the Old Testament, and from patristic works. The felicity of his translations sprang from his long study of English and Latin forms, as shown in his grammar, glossary and the *Colloquium*. Here the master questions the disciple as to his own work and that of his comrades: 'I am a professed monk', the disciple says: 'I sing seven times a day with the brethren and am occupied with reading and chant; but nevertheless, I would learn between whiles to speak in the Latin tongue'. His comrades have different occupations (which involves the use of a varied vocabulary in describing them): they include husbandmen, shepherds, oxherds, hunters, fishermen, fowlers, merchants, shoemakers, saltmakers and bakers! No such collection of people ever sat in a class with the disciple-monk: the *Colloquium* is an exercise in vocabulary, just as the *Hisperica Famina* were long before: but with a different aim: to give young monks an extensive knowledge of common Latin words.

The vigour and beauty of Ælfric's prose translations in some places rival those of Wycliffe and Tyndale. He was not dealing in the translations with the terms of abstract thought, like Alfred in his version of the *Consolation of Philosophy*, or Pecock later in his effort to write in English on theology: he could find the English equivalent of the Latin word, without having recourse to Anglicising a Latin one. In his gospel quotations in his homilies, as in his Old Testament

---

[1] Ælfric's identity has in the past been confused with that of Ælfric, archbishop of Canterbury, 995–1005, who was also a pupil of Æthelwold: he was renowned in his own day for holiness, but not for any scholarly writings. Ælfric's identity has also been mistakenly confused with that of Ælfric Bata, who copied and expanded a manuscript of the *Colloquium*, calling himself a pupil of abbot Ælfric who wrote it; Ælfric Bata may also have added an appendix to Ælfric's comment in Bede's *De temporibus*.

translations, the ranks and grades of people in the Bible were given their Anglo-Saxon equivalents, as Ælfric saw them. Christ is called the ætheling of God; Joseph in Egypt is reeve to Pharaoh, and the Israelites there were Welshmen (wealh meaning to the Anglo-Saxons both Welsh and slaves); since the English 'beadle' was also a herald John the Baptist becomes the beadle of Christ. The feasts of the patriarchs are called 'beer drinkings'. 'Publicans and sinners' became 'Reeves and sinful men'; the Saviour's disciples his 'learning knights'; the high priest, the ealdorbiscop; money, sceattas; the great men of Egypt are called Pharaoh's witan; the Lord went after this to a borough (byrig) called Capharnaum, and then there approached him a 'hundredes ealdor', praying him and saying: Lord, my knight (child) lieth at home bedridden. . . . Then the Saviour went to a certain borough, where a certain man was sitting at the toll-settle, called Matthew. . . . John the Baptist sent two learning-knights to Christ. . . . Then went he thence to the borough-shire that is called Tyre and the other that is called Sidon. . . . The apostles who have forsaken all and followed Christ shall, in the day when the Saviour sitteth on the settle of his majesty, sit on twelf doomsettles judging (giving dooms to) the twelve tribes of Israel. Of the centurion standing by the cross, he wrote: The hundred ealdor after these betokenings cried aloud: this is soothly God's bairn.

Ælfric's biblical translations were made at the pressing request of ealdorman Æthelweard. He made an English version of the earlier part of Genesis, and of selected passages from Numbers, Deuteronomy and Joshua. He had already given English outlines of the books of Kings and the Maccabees, and at some time of Judges, Esther, Job and Ruth.

Ælfric's selection of certain parts of the Old Testament for translation was conditioned by the fact that some Old Testament books were already translated, while the four gospels were already extant in a West Saxon version. Six manuscripts of this old version of the gospels exist, four of them written c. 1000 or between c. 1000 and c. 1050. Of all parts of the Bible the Gospels have been translated first into the vernacular in all countries, partly to render the gospels read at mass intelligible to unlearned priests, or literate lay people; the extant manuscript of Wulfila's Gothic gospels was, in fact, an altar book. Ælfric's work on the translation of the Old Testament accords with evidence that English gospels were already accessible to west countrymen.

Ælfric's translations of the Old Testament, though made at the request of a very learned layman, could hardly have reached a wide circle of lay people; but they would illuminate for the simpler monks the long readings from the scriptures at mattins. As used in a bishop's familia of strict canons, they might be used to instruct the young clerks in training in the school. There is no evidence as to how Æthelwold and his successors instructed young clerks at Winchester for the service of the see; no doubt the pastoral needs of the people of Winchester itself were met by the two churches of the Old and New Minsters; but against the background of Carolingian reform which demanded, as in the rule of Chrodegang, a school for young clerks, it is difficult to believe that Æthelwold made no provision for teaching them. Since the Benedictine rule, unlike that of Chrodegang, has no chapter about the maintenance of a school, there is no commentary about such a school in the *Concordia Regularis*: moreover, it was only the exceptional Benedictine minster that was the see church of a bishop. Though it would seem that some instruction must have been given to young clerics at Winchester, such instruction may have been informal: no evidence survives about such teaching.

Beside the biblical translations for Æthelweard, and Old Testament versions made at other times, Ælfric wrote for another noble layman, Sigwerth (c. 1006–1008), an *Introduction to the Old and New Testaments*, with many biblical quotations in English. It begins:

> Abbot Ælfric greeteth friendly Sigwerth at East Heolon. . . .
> Thou hast oft entreated me for English scripture, and I gave it thee not so soon, but thou first with deeds hast importuned me thereto, at which time thou didst so earnestly pray me for God's love to preach unto thee at thine own house: and when I was with thee, great moan thou madest that thou couldst get none of my writings. Now will I that thou have at least this little one sith knowledge is so acceptable to thee, and that thou wilt have it rather than be altogether without my books.

Ælfric then explains in his treatise, very shortly, the doctrine of the Holy Trinity and the Incarnation, and then deals with the book of Genesis, and the rest of the books of the Old and New Testaments, recounting their contents. One manuscript with the *Introduction* has then following an Old English version of Genesis, a rendering, of course, of the Vulgate. The first part of Genesis is accepted as Ælfric's work: the rest, and the following books, as an old version made before his day. Genesis begins:

In the beginning (on angynne) God made (gesceop) heaven and earth.

The earth truly was idle and empty, and darkness was over the breadth of the abyss, and God's spirit was borne over the waters.

And God said: let there be light: and light was made.

God saw that it was good: and he parted the light from the darkness.

Finally, Ælfric concerned himself not only with the instruction of his own monks and the enlightenment of laymen in the scriptures, but with the lives of the secular clergy. This appears in his two pastoral letters, one requested by bishop Wulfsige III of Sherborne (993–1001), his own bishop while he was at Cerne; and one for the bishop Wulfstan II of Worcester, who was also archbishop of York. Both letters had prefaces, and then sets of canons: both appear to have been originally in Latin, and supplied with English translations by Ælfric.[1]

To Wulfsige he wrote, in the Latin preface:

We have gladly yielded to your command, but we have not dared to write anything about the episcopal office, because it is for you to know how you ought to be by your good life an example to all men. . . . I say, however, that you ought very often to address your clergy and reprove their negligence, for through their perversity the statutes of the canons and the religion and teaching of holy church are almost completely destroyed. Now summon up your courage and tell them what priests and ministers of Christ ought to hold (observe), lest you perish yourself if you are accounted a dumb dog. We have indeed written this letter as if you were dictating it yourself (the 'dictate' suggests an address in a diocesan synod) and you were speaking to the clergy subject to you, beginning in this wise.

The first nine sections of the letter following teach the canonical requirement of celibacy of the clergy, and cite a canon of Nicea as

[1] See White, C. L., *Ælfric: a new study of his life and writings*, 1898: Yale Studies in English, ii, 135.

the first authority; there are 37 canons altogether, dealing with the obligations and work of the secular clergy, and the letter is indeed, in itself, a minor text-book on canon law, in English (see p. 126).

In the Latin preface of Ælfric's pastoral letter to bishop Wulfstan II (Ælfric's abbey of Eynsham was near to bishop Wulfstan's see of Worcester), he sends his greeting to archbishop Wulfstan and writes that he has translated into English two Latin letters that he had sent to Wulfstan the year earlier: not following the order exactly nor translating word for word but according to the sense. He hopes this will be profitable to some men and lead to their correction, though he knows it will be gravely displeasing to others: but it is not for us to be for ever silent on the subject and not to disclose to those subject to us the divine word: for if the herald be silent, who shall announce the coming of the judge?

The matter of the exhortation again is to priestly chastity, and it is implied that clerical marriage is common, is wrong, and that, though the archbishop may condemn it, he cannot enforce its discontinuance (see p. 135).

The other great homilist of the age, the Wulfstan to whom Ælfric addressed his *Sermo ad Sacerdotes*, appears to have come from the fenlands and been trained as a monk. Ely has been suggested as his monastery, but no Ely record mentions him as a brother of the house. He was however honoured there, and at Peterborough and the other great fenland abbeys; he belonged to the reformed Benedictine party. He succeeded Ælfstan in the see of London in 996[1] and had six years as bishop of this great trading city; then, in the latter part of 1002, he succeeded Ealdwulf as archbishop Wulfstan II of York, holding the see of Worcester in conjunction with York, like his two predecessors. There are few references to his work in the north, except as to the consecration of one or two bishops, for records in the north were few: no evidence connects him with the drawing up of the Law of the Northumbrian Priests (see p. 131). He was, however, often at the king's court, and he drew up many of the laws and signed many charters, both involving travel in all parts of England. He died at York in 1023 and was buried at Ely.

[1] See D. Whitelock's 'A note on the career of Wulfstan the homilist', EHR. lii (1936), 460.

It is now accepted that Wulfstan was the author of certain laws and canons once believed of earlier origin, of much of the legislation of the reigns of Æthelred and Cnut, and of some English homilies, including the famous *Sermo Lupi ad Anglos* (Wulfstan Latinised his name as Lupus).

His sermons were written in the desperate years of renewed Danish raids in king Æthelred's reign. The massacre on St. Brice's day occurred in 1002, the year when he was translated from London to York; in 1011 his fellow archbishop, Ælfheah of Canterbury, with whom he had presided over so many councils, was taken prisoner at the destructive Danish raid on Canterbury, and murdered the April following. In 1013 the Danish Swein was accepted as king of England, a visible sign of English defeat; king Æthelred had to flee for refuge to Normandy. Life was transitory, death and destruction near. So it had seemed to pope Gregory, writing with the Lombards at the gates of Rome: so it seemed to Wulfstan now. All good monks read Gregory's homilies and his book on Job: his thoughts lay at the back of Wulfstan's mind: had Gregory not written of this fugitive life as that of a man sailing upon a ship? 'For he that thus sails, stands or sits or lies: but ever he is borne onwards by the motion of the ship. So we, whether we wake or sleep, speak or keep silence, walk willingly or against our will, every day and in every moment of time we are borne forward towards our end.' 'Our present life', he wrote elsewhere, 'is as a puff of wind passing by; the Lord suffered on the sixth feria (Friday), and rested in the sepulchre on the seventh: and even so our present life is the sixth feria, for we lead it in sorrow and are tormented with miseries; the end cometh.' So Gregory: and Wulfstan wrote with an even sharper apprehension of final catastrophe.

Æthelred fled over sea in 1013: and Wulfstan wrote his *Sermo Lupi ad Anglos* when he had gone and before his return in 1014. The theme of the sermon is that calamities have so increased that we see that this world is hurrying to its end; Ælfric had written more than once that 'the end is near': now to Wulfstan it seems that the end of all things is assuredly at hand.

The sermon of the Wolf to the English when the Danes persecuted them most, which was in the year 1014 from the incarnation of our Lord Jesus Christ.

Beloved men, realise what is true: this world is in haste and the end approaches; and therefore in the world things go from bad to worse, and so it must of necessity deteriorate greatly on account of the people's sins before the coming of Antichrist, and indeed it will then be dreadful and terrible far and wide throughout the world.

Understand well also that now for many years the devil has led astray this people too greatly and there has been little loyalty among men, though they spoke fair enough; and too many wrongs prevailed in the land, and there were never many men who sought after a remedy as zealously as one should; but daily evil was piled on evil and wrongs and many lawless acts committed far too widely throughout all this people; also we have on that account suffered many losses and insults, and, if we are to experience any improvement, we must then deserve better of God than we have previously done. . . .

But it is true what I say, there is need of that relief, for God's dues have dwindled too long in every district within this nation, and the laws of the people have deteriorated all too much, and sanctuaries are violated far and wide, and the houses of God are entirely despoiled of ancient privileges and stripped inside of all that is seemly. And widows are wrongfully forced into marriage, and too many are reduced to poverty and greatly humiliated. And poor men are sorely deceived and cruelly defrauded and sold far and wide out of this country into the power of foreigners, although quite innocent; and children in the cradle are enslaved for petty theft by cruel injustice widely throughout this people. And the rights of freemen are withdrawn and the rights of slaves are restricted and charitable obligations are curtailed; and, in short, God's laws are hated and his precepts despised. And therefore we all through God's anger are frequently disgraced, let him perceive it who can; and this injury will become common to all this people, though one may not think so, unless God protect us.

For it is clear and manifest in us all that we have previously transgressed more than we have amended, and therefore much is assailing this people. Things have not gone well now for a long time at home or abroad, but there has been devastation and famine, burning and bloodshed in every district again and again; and stealing and killing, sedition and pestilence, murrain and disease, malice and hate and spoliation by robbers have harmed us very grievously, and monstrous taxes have afflicted us greatly, and bad seasons have very often caused us failure of crops. For now for many years, as it may seem, there have been in this country many injustices and wavering loyalties among men everywhere. . . .

Also we know well where that miserable deed has occurred that a father has sold his son for a price, and a son his mother, and one brother has sold another, into the power of strangers. And all these are grave and terrible deeds, let him understand who will. And yet, what is injuring this people is still greater and even more manifold; many are forsworn and greatly perjured, and pledges are broken again and again; and it is obvious in this people that God's anger violently oppresses us, let him perceive it who can. . . .

Alas for the misery, and alas for the public shame which the English now have, all through God's anger. Often two seamen, or maybe three, drive the droves of Christian men from sea to sea, out through this people, huddled together, as a public shame to us all, if we could seriously and rightly feel any shame. But all the insults which we often suffer we repay with honouring those who insult us; we pay them continually and they humiliate us daily; they ravage and they burn, plunder and rob and carry on board; and lo, what else is there in all these events except God's anger clear and visible over this people? . . .

There was a historian in the times of the Britons called Gildas, who wrote about their misdeeds, how with their sins they angered God so excessively that finally he allowed the army of the English to conquer their land and to destroy the host of the Britons entirely. . . . But let us do as is necessary for us, take warning from such; and it is true what I say, we know worse deeds among the English than we have heard of anywhere among the Britons; and therefore it is very necessary for us to take thought for ourselves and to intercede eagerly with God himself. And let us do as is necessary for us, turn to the right and in some measure leave wrong-doing, and atone very zealously for what we have done amiss; and let us love God and follow God's laws and perform very eagerly what we promised when we received baptism, or those who were our advocates at our baptism, and let us order our words and deeds rightly, and eagerly cleanse our thoughts, and keep carefully oath and pledge, and have some loyalty between us without deceit. And let us often consider the great Judgment to which we all must come, and save ourselves from the surging fire of hell torment, and earn for ourselves the glories and the joys which God has prepared for those who do his will in the world. God help us. Amen.[1]

Comparing Wulfstan's homilies with those of Ælfric; they have more fire and drive, though less finish and grace. He had a wide vocabulary, and whereas Ælfric heightened the poetical sense of his words by the old alliteration of the Anglo-Saxon poets, Wulfstan's passages show less alliteration, but a dramatic use of antithesis and particularly of doublets. The English used doublets (like sake and soke, etc.), but Wulfstan went far beyond the range of common expressions, and wrote of 'burning and bloodshed', 'harrying and hate' and the like. He lived in dramatic times: he used fine, dramatic English. There is good reason indeed to believe that beside writing fine prose, he was the author of the poems inserted into one text of the ASC. in the years 959 and 975, in praise of king Edgar.

The swing and vigour of Wulfstan's literary work, and many of the mannerisms of his style, appear also in the legal codes of Æthelred for the form of which he was responsible, and also in those of Cnut. Wulfstan was as anxious as any abbot to support the Benedictine reform: but he was an archbishop, not an abbot, and the pastoral care of all England, of Danes and Norsemen as well as Englishmen, was in his charge. He acted with the archbishops of Canterbury, but the wording of the codes of Æthelred which they instigated and approved seems to have been his own. He attended the king's witans, held more often in the south than in the north; his own North-umbrians were largely the descendants of Danish conquerors and settlers and not wholly converted from paganism; the reforming laws he drew up for Æthelred were more urgently needed in the north than in the south. Presumably more Christian war captives were sold abroad as slaves from Yorkshire than from Somerset.[2]

It is notable that laws dealing with Christians and their duty to the

---

[1] Quoted from Professor D. Whitelock's *English Historical Documents, c. 500–1042*, 855-859.

[2] See Robertson, A. J., *The Laws of the kings of England from Edmund to Henry I*, 1925, 78-107, and Whitelock, *Sermo Lupi ad Anglos*, 13-16.

church: with priests, clergy, monks and laity: were enacted in English at the witan, though apparently drafted by the two archbishops or Wulfstan himself. If they were discussed at any 'synod', meeting of the bishops and abbots alone, this must have been at a meeting preliminary to the witan, and there is no explicit reference to such. Wulfstan's first connexion with legislation appears to have been in 1008: Æthelred's Codes V and VI are varying versions of the statutes passed at Eanham in 1008. In addition to these two English versions, there is a Latin paraphrase, of which the preamble states that 'at that time it fell out that by the edict of king Æthelred, with the agreement of the archbishops Ælfheah and Wulfstan who suggested and urged it, all the nobles (optimates) of the English were summoned to meet on the holy day of Pentecost at the place called Eanham by the inhabitants'; and the Latin paraphrase ends with the words 'These lawful statutes and decrees were solemnly published in our synodal assembly by king (Æthelred), and all the nobles there present promised faithfully to obey them; therefore I, Wulfstan, by the grace of God archbishop of York, for the memory of those to come, and the salvation of those present and future, have written down these statutes (litteris infixi)'.

Two points about this code are notable. First, that a close connexion of matter and style has been established between it and the *Sermo Lupi ad Anglos*, written down years later, which supports the authorship asserted in the Latin paraphrase: Wulfstan would seem to have been responsible both for the English form published in the witan, and for the Latin version. A connexion is also accepted between Wulfstan's homilies and some of the later codes of Æthelred, and also some of Cnut's laws. Moreover, Wulfstan's authorship of the code once associated with the name of Dunstan,[1] and the laws once ascribed to Edward (the Elder) and Guthrum, is now generally accepted: he was a great law drafter.[2]

Secondly, that Codes V and VI, drawn up under the advice of the two archbishops, amount (in the first and longer part of the code) to a complete restatement of English law about the church. It is not called 'canon law', though the word canon does appear for the first time in a set of English laws; but the code opens with the general

[1] See K. Jost, 'The canons enacted under king Eadgar', in *Anglia*, Bd. 56 (1932), 288 following.
[2] See D. Whitelock, 'Wulfstan's Authorship of Cnut's Laws', in EHR. (1955), 72.

command that we must all honour and love God and observe the
Christian faith and renounce heathen practices, and goes on to cover
such matters as selling Christians as slaves, over heavy punishments,
monks out of monasteries, canons, priests who know they ought to
be celibate, marriage, church alms, burials, observance of feasts and
fasts, duties of the laity, and 'horrible perjuries and devilish deeds'
in general. In Code V, 25 of the 35 laws deal with church matters,
and the last 10 with secular matters and the defence of the realm; in
Code VI, the longer version, 30 of the 52 laws are ecclesiastical, the
last 22 secular. The wording of the last, the secular part, in each
version, suggests that it is an addendum: Code VI here has 'Further'.
It is possible that the draft of the ecclesiastical part had been approved
by the bishops first. However, the theory of canonical authority
behind the issue of canons by an archbishop or bishop was, in these
centuries, that the canons were issued on the authority of archbishop
or bishop, who had promulged or published them in the provincial
or diocesan synod: the sanction came from above, not from the
acceptance by the synod. If Ælfheah and Wulfstan drew up a set of
church laws, they were regarded as equally valid whether published
to the bishops in synod or the bishops and lay nobles in the witan;
the authority behind the archbishop's was, in any case, the king's.
Dunstan and Æthelwold and Wulfstan were strict reformers, zealous
for the rights of the church; there is no suggestion anywhere that
they desired the bishops to meet separately in ecclesiastical synod
and issue canons. The English crown was the best friend of the
reformers, and the only power that could, in fact, get anticlerical
ealdormen and thegns to accept them. The Blickling Homilies put
the king first in their notable phrase: 'the king and the bishop shall
be shepherds of Christian folk'.

The age of Ælfric and Dunstan was notable for the effort to
popularise learning, by the use of English exposition. Bede's exegetic
and scientific works were all in Latin: he could not hope to reach a
wider public than monks or monastically trained clergy. The Carolingians had popularised Latin learning by pressing for better educated
parish clergy, who should understand the Latin service books they
used. But the tenth century reformers in England preferred to use
the vernacular and reach not only the country clergy, but the lay
thegns and ealdormen (if they wished). They not only produced
English homilies and saints' lives, but translated technical Latin

treatises into English: they were not afraid even of tackling theology in English, which was a very different matter from making English versions of paraphrases of the scriptures: Ælfric, for instance, used theological exposition in some of the homilies and treatises.

As to English tracts produced now on technical and scientific subjects: an English calendar or martyrology was composed about A.D. 850 by translating an unknown Latin original, with recourse also to Bede's martyrology. Some scholar, perhaps Ælfric, turned Bede's *De temporibus* into English (c. 992), contributing some original material: any discussion of the calendar and method of determining Easter involved expounding astronomy according to the best knowledge of the day. About A.D. 1000 an English version of the spurious 'Letter of Alexander to Aristotle', with its description of India, was produced, and also two other romances for those interested in the Greek east, the *Apollonius of Tyre*, and the *Gospel of Nicodemus*, important as having first introduced into England the legend of Joseph of Arimathea and for its description of the descent of Christ into hell, which long influenced medieval art and drama. English tracts on medicine, herbs, healings and charms also appear: liberal minds did not consider it unsuitable to deal with any subject in English, and among such scholars, willing to incur some men's blame for rashness, was the monk, Byrhtferth of Ramsey, author of the (scientific) Manual or Encheiridion.

Æthelwold had founded the abbey of Ramsey in 970, and for two years his friend, Abbo of Fleury, had taught the school there: Byrhtferth described himself as the pupil of Abbo 'of venerable memory': he must have been writing after Abbo's death in 1004. He had himself travelled in France, for he mentions an observation on the length of shadows he had himself made at Thionville. He was 'scholasticus', teacher of the school, at Ramsey, and for the use of Latin-reading monks he wrote four Latin treatises enlarging on Bede's *De temporibus* and other works; but he also wrote in English the *Manual*, expounding the laws of astronomy and the calendar, for rustic priests, and, in English but more elaborately, for his young monks who had studied the first three liberal arts in Latin and were going on to study the four mathematical 'artes'; medieval studies followed the old Greco-Roman scheme.

Byrhtferth begins his *Manual*:

In the name of Christ I will begin this book. Here begins the computus of the Latins, Greeks, Hebrews, Egyptians and English. ... 'Computus' is in Greek 'ciclus' or 'rithmus'; according to the Egyptians it is called 'latercus' and according to the Macedonians 'calculus'. The Latins have twelve months, and likewise the Greeks, Hebrews, Egyptians and English.

He then states that the solar year has been skilfully investigated by our ancestors and proved to consist of three hundred and sixty-five days and a quarter; out of these days are made up the twelve months, consisting of two and fifty weeks. Then comes the explanation of the sidereal circle of the Zodiac, 'through which the sun and moon and the stars Saturn, Jupiter, Mars, Venus and Mercury run'. The sun completes its course through these twelve signs in twelve months; remaining in each sign for thirty days, ten hours and a half: an arithmetical discussion of the odd hours and half-hours follows, and of 'quadrants', and of intercalated or leap years. God fixed two solstices and two equinoxes (and when they occur). Then follows discussion of the four seasons, the four ages of man, the four humours, the four qualities. 'We have stirred with our oars the waves of a deep pool ... we have perceived the blossom of the lily (that is, the beauty of computation), we have scented the perfume of roses (that is, the profundity of reckoning). . . . These things we found at Ramsey . . . and I will not keep silence on account of the skill of scholars or for the sake of learned men who have no need to ponder there things among themselves . . . for we know of a surety that there are very many rustic clerks (in the Latin version, suburbani clerici) who do not know how many kinds of year there are, and I desire to instruct their ignorance, supported as I am by the patronage of the Fathers.'

The main body of this learned and intricate work follows, and Byrhtferth deals, still in Anglo-Saxon, not only with astronomy and divisions of time, but with science as he knew it: with the sun and planets, the atom, the days of the week each made a feria or holy day by bishop Sylvester, Sunday becoming feria prima, Monday feria secunda, etc. 'We could add many things here,' Byrhtferth continues, 'but forasmuch as we know that these things seem sufficiently complex to clerks and upland priests, we will now direct our words to the young monks, who have occupied their childhood with scientific books. . . . We have set down in this manual many things about the computus, because we wished that young men should be able the more easily to understand the Latin and speak with greater freedom to old priests about these things. . . . In the next place, we intend to address the young pupils of the monastery. . . . We implore scholars and educated men, who know these things perfectly, not to be annoyed with these things which in our imperfect fashion we set down and serve up to young boys.' Part III, which follows, deals yet more thoroughly with the 'Pascha', the cycle of nineteen years, which is very difficult to expound in English: Byrhtferth bids heathen authorities and inspirations begone: depart, ye sirens and Castalian nymphs and Phoebus, whom Latona bore to Apollo in Delos, 'as ancient triflers have declared': may the golden cherubim bring from the heavenly altar a spark of burning coal to touch the nerves of his dumb mouth, that he may translate this cycle into English in scholarly fashion. He concludes the prayer by translating into English two lines of the hymn beginning:

Spiritus alme veni! sine te non diceris unquam:

the first English hymn, 'Come, Holy Ghost', was thus written[1] as an invocation to help explain the computus. The exposition is indeed elaborate, with another diagram of interlocked circles, and various tables: the scribe's skill in illumination was made to serve the cause of scientific explanation.

Although the great innovation of the reformers of this age was the use of English prose, it is not to be supposed that the old English poetry went unvalued. It was a medium that could be handed down in men's memories: English song could be still sung at feasts: but some manuscripts survive which are collections of English poetry only. The writing of manuscripts was expensive: but some patrons thought it fitting that such a costly codex of poetry should be made. One such collection, written about 1000, had *Beowulf*, the *Wonders of the East*, the *Letter of Alexander to Aristotle*, and the story of *Judith* told in the Old English heroic manner. The more famous *Exeter Book*, given to the minster of Exeter by bishop Leofric, is the greatest surviving codex of Old English poems, including old, heroic poems

---

[1] It runs in Anglo-Saxon: Cum nu, Halig Gast, butan the ne bist thu gewurdod, and is not, of course, an ancestor of the familiar English version of the 'Veni creator spiritus',

like the *Wanderer* and the *Seafarer*, the poems of Cynewulf, and those of the tenth century like *The Judgment Day* and the *Descent into Hell*. The *Vercelli Book* also was written in England, probably by a single scribe, and contains both prose homilies and poems like the *Andreas*, the *Fates of the Apostles*, the *Elene* and the *Dream of the Rood*; the homilies would probably have been read in refectory, and the presence of the poems in the same codex gives rise to wonder whether they also were so read.

CHAPTER V

CHURCH SERVICE BOOKS: THE GELASIAN, GALLICAN, GREGORIAN AND CAROLINGIAN SACRAMENTARIES, AND THEIR USE IN ENGLAND

WHILE there are few surviving liturgical manuscripts of English provenance dating from the seventh to the tenth centuries, no evidence suggests that they differed in kind from those used elsewhere in western Europe; liturgical history and specially that of the consecration of bishops and coronation of kings in England has to be inferred from Continental evidence and analogy.

The history of the old service books in the Carolingian empire was found to affect liturgical practice in England; there was still no single, imposed, book of the sacraments, and the only attempt to secure liturgical conformity was made, not by a pope, but by the emperor Charles the Great: and it failed. It is unlikely that liturgical practice in England differed much from that among the Franks before Charles's effort to secure conformity with Roman practice. Both sides of the Channel the old Gelasian sacramentary was receiving various accretions from Gallican or Irish sources (for Columbanus' followers made Irish influence as strong among the Franks as among the English): among the Franks only, however, Visigothic influence spread in the south, especially after the Muslim conquest of Spain brought Visigothic refugees and salved manuscripts to south France and Italy. Irish and the old Gallican practice was however the more pervasive. The arrangement of the calendar, beginning from New Year's day, as in the Gregorian sacramentary, was increasingly used; but in its pastoral and priestly character, its blessings and its occasional offices, the sacramentary used by the Franks and the English was the Gelasianum.

The most famous example of a Frankish sacramentary, the one known as the *Missale Francorum*,[1] was a manuscript in the uncial script, written in the neighbourhood of Poitiers about 700 to 750:

[1] Vat. MS. Reg. latin 257: see Ellard, 18.

66

it was written under Visigothic influence, and contains the first direction for the anointing of the hands of the priest at ordination (the anointing of the dying was much earlier). The bishop here had no anointing. It is a Gallican service book with formularies unquestionably Roman in origin: and there must have been many sacramentaries like it.

Another famous manuscript of the Frankish Gelasian sacramentary, written c. 750 in the Amiens–Paris–Soissons area and in the script of the abbey of Corbie, is a Gelasian sacramentary showing the influence of Irish and Anglo-Saxon manuscripts.[1] It has the blessing of the Paschal Candle, showing that Gallican additions to the Paschal rite were read from a separate book: the rubric enjoins that after this ceremony 'he says the prayers contained in the (Gelasian) sacramentary'. There is no anointing of the bishop: a matter to be, in the century following, of political as well as liturgical importance; the bishop, in this Gallican book, is not yet a 'christus domini'.

Sacramental anointing, however, was to be increasingly used: Pepin the Short was anointed king by St. Boniface, and again by pope Stephen. The anointing of the bishop's head appears for the first time in the manuscript[2] long known as the 'sacramentary of Gellone', and now known by liturgists as an example of the Eighth century Gelasian books.

This 'Eighth century Gelasian' has a martyrology showing it was written for the abbey of Rebais near Meaux, and about the years 750 to 780. Here the priest at ordination was clothed for the first time with the chasuble as sacerdotal (at Rome all clerks wore it); and at ordination oil was poured on the bishop's head. This was the most notable innovation. No example of an Eighth century Gelasian of English origin has survived, but there is no reason to suspect that they differed greatly from those used by the Franks. English surviving manuscripts of the period were preserved for their beautiful illumination, and the most beautifully illuminated books were gospel books.

Charles the Great, who had extended the empire of the Franks by the conquest of Germany beyond the Rhine and of the Lombards in north Italy, was a lover of uniformity. He requested from Rome a codex of the canon law as used there under papal authority, and

[1] Vat. MS. 316A: see *ib.* 23.
[2] MS. Bibl. Nat. Paris 12048: see Ellard, 29.

from Monte Cassino a copy of the Benedictine rule. He also commissioned Paul the Deacon to ask at Rome for a copy of the Roman
mass book; this would include not only the masses for the course of
the year, but those used on special occasions, such as ordinations, etc.
The Roman use was, in fact, very ancient, very brief and very
severe; when the abbot John of Ravenna between 784 and 791
brought the desired copy to Charlemagne, a 'Gregorian' sacramentary, the Gallican prelates were amazed, not at what it contained,
but at what it did not contain. Since it was barely possible to impose
the use of the book as it was on all the Frankish bishops, Charles
commissioned Alcuin to write an official supplement to the Roman
book, to satisfy at least in part those long used to Gallican additions
to the liturgy. The use of the Roman sacramentary was made
obligatory in Charles's dominion: the use of Alcuin's supplement in
addition was left a matter of choice. When Alcuin's supplement, his
selection from the Frankish books, was completed, only the Roman
book and the supplement were to be used throughout the Carolingian empire, at Charles's order. All altars were to have a copy of it,
and the original, the 'authenticum', was to be kept in the palace
library at Aix. No such sweeping measure had ever been attempted;
the papacy had safeguarded its own use, but had been notably chary
in sending copies elsewhere, even at the request of kings.

The new book required a great simplification of ceremonial, as
well as omitting ceremonies at ordinations to which the Franks were
long used. The now-enjoined Roman ordination had no anointing
of the priest's hands, no investing of the new priest by the bishop
with the chasuble: all alike in the great procession wore the chasuble.
The bishop was not anointed. Alcuin retired to his abbey of Tours
in 796, to his little house in the abbey grounds where the cuckoo
sang, and got on with his supplement, copies of which were made
and issued between 797 and 800. But the new book never really
replaced the Eighth century Gelasian, copies of which continued to
be written well after 800: they were made in Nivelles (Belgium),
Reichenau, Saint-Gall, Echternach, Cologne, Monza, and many
other notable scriptoria. In general, the new Roman book with its
supplement became fused with the old Frankish sacramentaries: the
Franks found it, even with the Alcuinian supplement (in modern
language), too Puritan. A catalogue made in 831 at Angilbert's great
abbey of Saint-Riquier lists, in the 'sanctuary books used for the

service of the altar', three Gregorian missals (the new Roman book), a 'Gregorian and Gelasian missal drawn up in modern times by Alcuin', and nineteen Gelasian missals.

The Gelasian mass book was quite generally met with a full half-century after its official banishment among the Franks; various ninth century abbeys had copies of it, and various small country churches; Walafrid Strabo, abbot of Reichenau and a scientific liturgist, wrote in a booklet of 840–842 of the widespread use of the Gelasian sacramentary. But at the same time, Charles's mass book and supplement was being copied and used, at first with some small additional supplements from the Eighth century Gelasian, and later with very large borrowings.

In the reigns of Louis the Pious and Charles's descendants, the old-fashioned lack of uniformity was resumed. Royal control of the liturgy lapsed in the family wars of the Carolingians. Louis the Pious carried through his legislation about monks and canons, using Helisachar his chancellor as a guide for the new regulations about secular canons. Such canons served cathedrals and bishops and needed guidance about service books: Helisachar gave a supply of service books from the palace at Aix to Amalarius of Metz, pupil of Alcuin, to deal with the matter. Among the books Amalarius used was Isidore of Seville's *De ecclesiasticis officiis*, and Amalarius set about producing an up-to-date book on the subject. By 827 he had become bishop of Metz, and he presented Louis with his newly written *De ecclesiasticis officiis libri iv*, which became a standard text-book and commentary on liturgical rites (see p. 70). Its chief importance at the date was the quasi-official recognition it gave to the older, Frankish ceremonial: he borrowed from Isidore of Seville the description in Exodus xxix. 4, 9, of the vesting and anointing of Aaron and his sons as 'sacerdotes'. Helisachar and Amalarius thus propounded the biblical image of the priesthood and its inception to justify departure from the authenticum, then lying in the book chest at Aix. In ordinations he provided that the hands of the priest and the head of the bishop should be anointed: on the other hand, he denied that the holding of a gospel book by two bishops over the head of the bishop to be consecrated had any ancient authority; though it had actually been prescribed in the *Missale Francorum*, the old Gelasian, and the Eighth century Gelasian. (It survived in later English pontificals.)

In the disturbed ninth century, when bishops themselves were occasionally set upon and murdered, any additional sanctity that could be attached to a bishop's person was welcome; the Forged Decretals of 847–852 enjoined the anointing of the bishop's head, coupling with it the verse 'Touch not mine anointed'. The verse with its implications was relevant also for the anointing of kings. Some Frankish bishops were in not unreasonable doubt as to whether an anointing should be given at the ordination of priests and deacons, and archbishop Rudolf of Bourges wrote to inquire of pope Nicholas I; Amalarius enjoined such anointing and the anointing of the bishop: the Forged Decretals (accepted for the most part) stressed it: Rudolf inquired about privately consecrated coadjutor bishops. Pope Nicholas answered:

> Moreover, you have asked, whether priests alone or deacons as well, should have their hands anointed with the chrism, when they are ordained. In neither case in the holy Roman church which by the grace of God I serve is this done. Nor do we read, unless our memory fails us, that the ministers of the new Law (a tacit reference to Amalarius and Aaron) have ever had this done to them.

Moreover, pope Nicholas sent Rudolf a copy of a letter of pope Innocent I, sternly rebuking those who introduced liturgical novelties, and bidding him, if he wished to preserve apostolic tradition intact, to shun diversity and variety in ordinations and consecrations.

Nevertheless, in ninth century France, it was old custom and the text-book of Amalarius, not the conservative Roman tradition of liturgy, that prevailed, as is exemplified in a sacramentary of the early tenth century written at Corbie, which is a mixture of the Eighth century Gelasian and the Caroline book: it has the anointing of the priest's hand, and the bishop's head, and from such a source the missals and pontificals of the tenth century were derived, both in France and England. The extension of the Cluniac influence to Rome, the visits of abbot Odo of Cluny, the establishment of the new monasticism at Monte Cassino, Subiaco, Farfa and other Italian centres, brought with it the extension of the Frankish rites to Italy. Anointing had come to Rome by way of Ravenna in the time of pope John X; the Frankish ceremonial, as more splendid, had tended to spread from one liturgical centre to another, and now in the tenth century it had reached Rome. Stamped with the Roman mark, it went out again to the farthest corner of Latin Christendom. Later in the tenth century the chief influence on liturgical history was to be that of Dunstan and his followers in England.

Among the sacraments in the new service books of the tenth century, that of the anointing of the king was to have great political importance, both to church and state. It introduced a new concept of kingship to the Anglo-Saxons: it linked England with Carolingian practice, and it enhanced the political power of the clergy as the administrators of the anointing, a position which fell to them naturally, and also as the agents in the conferment of the regalia, etc., a part which might equally have been performed by laymen. In Dr. Schramm's words: 'The eighth century combined the Christian rite of anointing with the Teutonic inauguration. The tenth century added coronation and investiture by ecclesiastics and fixed the pattern of the coronation service.'[1]

The tribal kings of the Celts, and the Germanic ones who invaded Europe mainly in the fifth century, all assumed the kingship with some ceremony of inauguration, carried through with at least a dual intention. The new king must become possessed of the magical powers of his predecessor, as necessary to his office, and he must assume royal powers publicly, by some well known ceremony, that his people may know that he is king. The Merovingian kings, whose long hair testified to their royal and magical power, passed round the frontiers of their kingdom in an ox cart, visibly inaugurating a new reign. Among the northern nations, the royal heir was placed on the chief seat in the royal hall: among warlike tribes, he was raised on the shield: for centuries the seating of a new king on the throne took place at a royal banquet. Among the Irish, and some northern nations, the new king must walk to a stone, or seat himself upon a hillock, both representing the mound or tumulus of the ruler's predecessor, whose magical powers would pass thence to his successor. The Scots borrowed from the Irish this form of inauguration, making the new monarch sit upon a stone (Charles II was thus actually crowned king of the Scots at Scone before he was crowned king of England). Among the Germanic nations the use of a special

[1] *A history of the English coronation rite*, Schramm, P. E., trans. Wickham Legg, L. G., 1937, 73.

sword and the wearing of a golden helmet were associated with the inauguration of a new king, and they survived to become associated with the Christian rite of anointing in the tenth century. The Anglo-Saxon bretwalda, the war-leader, the sharpener of swords, had his symbolic whetstone, of which a specimen was interred at Sutton Hoo: but this symbolic royal instrument fell out of use before the Christian inauguration rite was formulated.

The practice of anointing a new king was adopted after acceptance of Christianity had given rise to a desire to Christianise the half-magical inaugural ceremonies of Celts and Anglo-Saxons. The reference by Gildas to the scriptural anointing of Saul by Samuel does not show that Celtic kings before Gildas were anointed, but it shows the traditional half-magical powers of the king were felt to be providential in a Christian dispensation, and the Old Testament blessing with oil was cited as evidence of it; the Welsh kings mentioned, Gildas writes, have done frightful things, and these crimes are the worse in that kings have done them.

In 751 the Franks adopted the blessing with anointing as a special form of royal consecration, and the solemn act was not unnoticed in England. In 781 two sons of Charlemagne were anointed in their father's life-time by the pope, and in 785 king Offa had his son Ecgfrith anointed and raised upon a throne. From this time all Anglo-Saxon rulers, it would seem, received the church's 'ordinatio' or consecratio; the pope had solemnly crowned Charlemagne emperor in 800, and the Carolingian kings who succeeded to parts of his empire were also anointed and crowned: the coronation rite or 'ordo' developed and became recognised as consisting of certain necessary parts. Archbishop Hincmar of Reims (d. 883), scholar, palaeographer and liturgist, played the leading part in this development; the old Germanic tribal king, inaugurated by a traditional ceremony, became under the Carolingians a 'christus domini', guarded by the biblical sanction, 'touch not mine anointed'.

All this did not pass unobserved in England. King Egbert of Wessex (802–838) had passed three years in exile in Frankland before he became king of Wessex and raised her to the leading position earlier held by Mercia. His son Æthelwulf (839–856) also admired the Carolingian tradition: he sent his young son Alfred to Rome in 853, where the pope gave him consular insignia. Succeeding as he did in the middle of a desperate military conflict,

Alfred was 'chosen to king' without, so far as any evidence shows, any anointing or coronation. His father Æthelwulf had caused his second wife, Judith, to be anointed and crowned at their marriage in 856: Hincmar of Reims had drawn up the ordo for the ceremony, for up till this point no wife of an English king had been crowned. The Anglo-Saxon word 'cwen' meant merely 'wife': otherwise the royal consort would be merely termed 'lady' (hlædige). Henceforth she would be indeed 'regina'. But both these instances of assimilation of Anglo-Saxon to Frankish practice were isolated examples: the fifty years of Danish wars interrupted such assimilation, and only after the mid tenth century did it begin again.

At king Edmund's accession in 940 the Frankish practice of making an oath of loyalty or allegiance was adopted; in England the king had been regarded as responsible for the preservation of peace, the removal of wrong-doing and the establishment of justice: but no promise had been made either by the king or his subjects at his inauguration or anointing. Meanwhile, on the Continent, the emperor Henry I had refused to be anointed at his accession in 919, on the ground that the clergy should not concern themselves with politics; but Otto I had had himself solemnly anointed and crowned at Aix in 936. The ordo used at his coronation was combined with an old Frankish ordo at Mainz in 961, and this full and rich ordo became the norm for German coronation ordines in future. The strengthening of the king's power by a solemn assimilation of his 'ordination' to that of priest and bishop was in the air in the mid tenth century; the charters of Anglo-Saxon kings far earlier had described them as 'ruling by divine grace' or 'divine favour', but the new coronation rites stressed the divine and providential character of their rule.

Up till the reign of Edgar (959–975) there had been no fixed ordo for the anointing or coronation of an English king. He was 'chosen to king' by the witan on Eadwig's death in 959: and it was after long pondering and liturgical study that Dunstan solemnly anointed and crowned him in 973, in the year when he became thirty years old. The long deferment of the anointing seems connected with the quasi-sacerdotal character now conferred on the king, and the care with which the new ordo was drawn up is indicated by the fact that one or two experimental drafts were made before the one actually used. A great impression was made on Edgar's subjects, and the

6

Parker Chronicle (a version of the ASC. kept till the eleventh century in the Old Minster at Winchester) breaks into verse under the year 973:

> In this year Edgar, ruler of the English,
> Was consecrated king by a great assembly
> In the ancient city of Acemannesceaster,
> Also called Bath by the inhabitants
> Of this island. On that blessed day,
> Called and named Whit Sunday by the children of men
> There was great rejoicing by all.

Dunstan, when he prepared for the long delayed coronation of Edgar in 973, had no established Anglo-Saxon formularies to follow. He could and did however follow certain Frankish ones; archbishop Hincmar of Reims had produced more than one coronation rite, and his anointing and coronation of Charles the Bald at Metz in 869 had been a splendid ceremony. Hincmar's rites were studied in England.

For the coronation of Edgar in 973 at least three draft schemes appear to have been made, or to have been used for an earlier coronation. The rite accepted as that actually used in 973 appears in a manuscript[1] often described as the pontifical of St. Dunstan, though actually written shortly after Dunstan's death for bishop Wulfsige III of Sherborne; the same coronation rite written out in the manuscript was copied into the sacramentary of abbot Ratoaldus of Corbie (d. 986), and was thence somewhat widely copied among the Franks. In addition to the formularies in these four recensions, we have a lively account of the coronation of 973 and the banquet afterwards, given by the monk of Ramsey.

The three earlier schemes, or draft coronation schemes, appear in the Leofric missal, the Lanalet pontifical and the pseudo-Egbert pontifical (see pp. 76-84).

[1] Paris, Bibl. Nat. MS. latin, 943: see Omont, *Catalogue*, and Ellard, 78-79.

CHAPTER VI

THE TENTH CENTURY REFORM: LITURGY:
ART: ARCHITECTURE

THE revival of Benedictine monasticism in the tenth century was accompanied, naturally enough, by a renaissance of liturgical study, the illumination of manuscripts and a new style in sculpture and church building. The monks of Winchester, Glastonbury, Ramsey and the other refounded abbeys copied liturgical manuscripts, expressed their devotion in holy week and Easter with new ceremonies and processions, and re-edited their sacramentaries. Since the latter were now large and compendious volumes, the monks wrote for use in chapel a number of smaller liturgical books; separate gospel books for the altar had long been in use, and to these were now added epistle books, collectars, tropers (song books: books with the sequences), grails (graduals: other music books for the mass, with the verses of the psalm to be sung before the gospel), antiphoners (with the music for the divine office), calendars, martyrologies and books of blessings (benedictionals). The new monasteries needed new buildings and churches and books for their sacristies and book chests. Beautiful altar books were much valued, and perhaps of all the arts that of manuscript illumination received the greatest impetus.

The history of the sacramentaries used in England from the age of Theodore till that of Edward the Confessor is no longer one merely of inference and deduction: there are surviving manuscripts. The sacramentaries, general books of rites and blessings, tended to be replaced by pontificals and missals. Lesser liturgical books were also written and a few have survived, or are mentioned in surviving catalogues. There are few surviving English manuscripts, however, from the period of the Danish raids, c. 850–900; what happened in English churches must here be inferred mainly from a Carolingian background; but the tenth century brought the rebuilding of church life and an impetus to all the crafts ancillary to monastic life.

The Benedictine life hung upon liturgical practice throughout the year, and lent itself to liturgical study: the English monks had access to and studied the service books of Corbie or Reims and the other Frankish abbeys, as also the *Ordines Romani*.[1] When an abbot or bishop ordered a service book to be written, however, the scribe seldom limited himself to copying one manuscript only; he combined liturgical material of different dates and places of origin, sometimes adding a form of prayer or blessing from a house quite other than that of his main manuscript source, sometimes adding prayers or blessings from different sources at a particular point in the rite. Liturgical development, even in a particular house, was never stationary.

The old sacramentaries had included not only calendars and masses, but many 'sacramental' forms (like the blessing of chrism, or holy water) which were not as sharply marked off from sacraments as later. In the age of Dunstan books were written for the use of bishops (called by modern liturgists pontificals and benedictionals), or for priests, called missals, but they were still general books. Both pontificals and missals would normally include calendars (for local observance), the year's masses, and special masses, and probably old forms for sacraments and sacramentals; for instance, the first part of the Leofric missal is, in fact, an Eighth century Gelasian book, with the Caroline Gregorian, and Alcuin's supplement, together with some more modern occasional offices; it had also the office for the dedication of a church, which only a bishop could perform. A pontifical by definition should contain only episcopal rites: but the distinctive mark of a pontifical or benedictional is, in fact, that it contains the episcopal blessings given only by the bishop at mass before the administration of communion (see p. 82): it may contain much else.

Among the surviving manuscripts of English rites written in this age, the following are the most important. Of the pontificals, the Lanalet Pontifical and the so-called Pontifical of Egbert,[2] both of which have the episcopal blessings at communion, together with many other rites, including the coronation rite; the Benedictional of Æthelwold, a much shorter though beautifully illuminated manu-

---

[1] For a translation of the text of an early ordo of a pontifical mass at Rome, see Atchley, F. G. C. F., *Ordo Romanus Primus*, 1905: in the Library of Liturgiology and Ecclesiology for English Readers, vol. vi.

[2] Written c. 1000 and used at Évreux in Normandy; see Ellard, 80.

script, containing only the episcopal blessings at mass as they followed the course of the liturgical year; and the so-called 'pontifical of St. Dunstan'[1] actually written at the end of the tenth century, probably for bishop Wulfsige III (Wulfsin) of Sherborne, 992–1001; it has the letter of pope John XII to Dunstan, accompanying the sending of the pallium, and also one to bishop Wulfsige. The manuscript gives the Canterbury usage just after Dunstan's death.

Of the missals, the Leofric missal, written in Lotharingia early in the tenth century, is a mine of information, not only for the calendar and a form of the coronation rite, but for the occasional offices; the missal of Robert of Jumièges, written at Winchester before Robert was made bishop of London in 1051 and acquired by him; and the Red Book of Derby, which was written shortly after 1061, at some monastery in the diocese of Winchester, probably, from internal evidence, the New Minster, are also important sources.

The 'pontifical of Egbert' (archbishop of York 732–766)[2] survives in a Paris manuscript written c. 950–1000; in this and other manuscripts it is found associated with a penitential ascribed to Egbert, but actually of later date. The pontifical, apparently put together in the age of Dunstan, has a very old litany of the saints, of north country provenance: St. Cuthbert and St. Guthlac of Croyland (floruit c. 700) are invoked, but no saints of later date; the Merovingian St. Médard is also invoked. The offices in the pontifical include that of confirmation, the ordination of the various orders of clergy, beginning with the exorcist, the consecration of an altar, the dedication of a church, and many blessings for special seasons or occasions: the exaltation of the holy cross, the veiling of a nun, prayers against lightning, etc. The office for the ordination of a bishop is of interest: both his head and his hands are anointed (see p. 67), 'fundat super eum benedictionem'; and, as part of the ceremony, two bishops hold the gospel book over his head. The anointing of bishops was certainly practised in England at this time: a charter of 963 speaks of bishop Oswald of Worcester as a bishop 'ordained with the chrism of Christ'.[3]

[1] MS. Bibl. Nat. Paris latin 943; see Ellard, 78; Lauer, Bibl. Nat. Catal. général des manuscrits latins, I, no. 943.

[2] For a translation, see *The Pontifical of Egbert, archbishop of York*, published in 1853 as vol. xxvii of the Surtees Soc.; the information about the history of the pontifical is out of date; see Ellard, 80.   [3] ASChar., 65.

The Lanalet pontifical[1] also belongs to the period of the tenth century reform and is of special interest as an episcopal book for the west of England showing both Celtic and Carolingian influence: and also for the many pastoral prayers and blessings affecting lay people, from the blessing of a font to masses for the reconciliation of a church (after bloodshed, fighting in it, etc.) and prayers at the ordeal of hot iron. The manuscript of the Lanalet pontifical, now at Rouen, was once in the possession of the abbey of Jumièges; it was written in the tenth century and was compiled for an English bishop; its English origin is shown by some Anglo-Saxon words in the manuscript, and blessings for Anglo-Saxon saints' days. St. Birinus, the apostle of Wessex, is invoked, and St. Andrew, the patron of Wells cathedral; the book must have been used at Wells, for a blessing for use on St. Andrew's day has the words: 'You have received St. Andrew as your special patron' (after St. Cyngar). There is another blessing for St. Cuthbert's day, and St. Cuthbert was early venerated at Wells, and an early parish church there is dedicated to him. The pontifical has nevertheless become known as the Lanalet Pontifical because it has a form of excommunication said to be used by 'the bishop of the monastery of Lanalet', the Cornish minster with the Celtic place name which was later known as St. Germans. This monastery-bishopric was made a territorial see by king Athelstan c. 930, Conan becoming bishop; his name is Celtic, and he may have been abbot-bishop there before. The book is that of a Wessex bishop, but only the excommunication form comes from St. Germans. A marginal note in the manuscript says that it was the book of Lyfing, bishop of Crediton (and Cornwall) till 1047.

The pontifical is written in different hands and its foundation is the Gregorian sacramentary with the Alcuinian supplement; much else is added.[2] The contents include a form of dedication for a church, a litany with some Frankish saints (St. Geneviève, St. Remigius of Reims, etc.), some Irish saints venerated in Gaul (St. Brigid and St. Columbanus), and 'an order how relics are laid up in the holy Roman church'. Since most churches now dedicated to a patron saint would have relics of the saint laid up beneath or before

[1] For the text, see G. H. Doble's *Pontificale Lanaletense*, 1937, and for information, his *The 'Lanalet Pontifical'*, 1934.

[2] A reference to a 'cardinal deacon' comes from the *Ordines Romani*; see *Pont. Lanal.*, supra, p. 12.

the altar, relics which might be personal or merely cloths which had lain touching the tomb of the martyr in Rome, or some city of Gaul or the East; this rite for the deposit of relics might well be seen by lay people once in a life-time. The pontifical lays down that the bishop goes to the place where the relics have rested the night before, with vigil kept, and he raises the relics while a litany is sung and he prays; and priests bear the bier (feretrum) with the relics to the church with due honour; and with many crosses and censers and taperers with lighted candles and with thanks to God and with antiphons. The bishop enters the church with prayer to God who invisibly contains all things and yet for man's salvation shows visibly the signs of his power (miracles often occurred during the translation of relics): he takes the relics from the priest, and with his own hands hides them 'in the confession of the altar', together 'with three portions of the consecrated host and three grains of incense'; they are enclosed with the relics of the saints. The holy oil is poured on the new altar and a cross made at its four corners; the altar is veiled and antiphons sung: 'Terrible is this place, for it is the house of God and the gate of heaven'. The veneration of relics was indeed a part of English pre-Conquest religion; to the villager, the saint and life after death, and the saint's continued protection of those who asked his or her help, were almost commonplace certainties: at any juncture they might call on God to intervene. Miracles were very joyful signs of the kindness of God, and never out of place or out of expectation. To such faith the church extended her blessing.

But more than this, the church was always concerned with the keeping of the peace, and in Anglo-Saxon society where there was no police force, the sanctity of the oath was of great importance. A man swore the old hold oath of loyalty to his thegn; oath breach was a grave offence and any circumstance that strengthened such a sanction was to be welcomed. The oath was binding; swearing upon the relics of the saints was trebly binding, for it was swearing before the living saint in heaven, who was likely to punish the breach of such an oath. The veneration of relics was encouraged by the pastoral church for various reasons, some worthy, some financial and less worthy: but among them all, the desire to prevent oath breach was powerful and commendable. Swearing on the gospels was not yet practised: at the great Domesday inquest of 1086 all the jurors (those giving sworn evidence) swore on the relics.

To return to the Lanalet pontifical. After the office for the dedication of a church comes the mass of reconciliation of a church desecrated, where the bishop makes the circuit of the church with the clergy singing the litany and praying that the Lord will turn again and show mercy to this church 'consecrated to his name and prepared for the sacraments but violated by deceitful and diabolic infestation'.

Then comes (out of any logical order) the form for the coronation of a queen by bishop or priest: she is given a ring, and crowned with the words 'Receive the crown of glory and honourable joyfulness: that thou mayest be crowned by the lord with eternal exultation' (see p. 73). Then follows the consecration of a virgin and her habit: and a form where a widow is blessed and given a 'pallium'. Then the forms for the giving of the tonsure to a clerk, the blessing of monks, and the offices for blessing the ostiarius, lector, acolyte, exorcist, sub-deacon, deacon, priest: with a rubric that a cantor (lector), after he has been instructed by the archdeacon (the head deacon in a bishop's familia), may receive this 'office of singing' at the command of the priest alone (no episcopal sanction being required); the deacon's hand is anointed; the priest is given a stole, the special title to a church, the blessing of the bishop and the priests assisting, and an anointing of his hand and his head (see p. 69): he is clothed with the chasuble.

In the ordination of a bishop, it is laid down that two bishops shall hold the gospel book over his head, his head shall be anointed and his hands; he shall receive the sevenfold blessing of the spirit, the staff of the pastoral office and the ring; and he shall be led to the episcopal chair (cathedra).

The Lanalet pontifical has also a rite for the solemn blessing of the king, and possibly an earlier one than that used by Dunstan for the coronation of Edgar at Bath in 973. If so, it is the first surviving rite for the distinctive English series of royal blessings and anointings, and perhaps earlier than the so-called pontifical of Egbert, with which it has interesting points of comparison. It was especially important to the tenth century reformers to stress the sacred character of kingship; the king was the great champion of monks and enemy of secular, hereditary control of minsters, whether the claim to keep the abbacy in the patron's family, to have a son of the married canon succeed, when ordained, to his father's prebend, or (more frequent still) to keep as laymen lands once leased out by king or abbot when the minster needed defence from the Danes, or lay desolate after pillaging. It was very necessary to stress the difference between the king and the secular kin of the founders and patrons of the old minsters; to stress that when the king exercised his right to appoint abbots and bishops, it was no mere layman who thus selected (or approved the monastic selection of) the church's hierarchy, but one who by special anointing and blessing was half an ecclesiastic himself.

The order for the 'blessing of a king newly elected' in the Lanalet pontifical is not technically that for a coronation, for a helmet is placed upon the king's head, and not a crown. Other old pagan ceremonies for the inaugural of a tribal or royal ruler are also included. The order has a prayer that God will grant peace in the king's borders and no evil beast nor the sword of an enemy cross his boundaries: the king is anointed and the bishops sing the antiphon, 'Zadoc the priest and Nathan the prophet anointed Solomon in Zion, and they that rejoiced cried: Let the king live for ever'. The bishops and the princes put a sceptre into his hand, singing a long, scriptural blessing; they put a rod (baculus) into his hand, with prayer; all the bishops place a helmet (galea) on his head, and then they bless the prince and all the people cry aloud three times with the bishops and the princes, Let the king live for ever, and all the people come to kiss the prince (ad osculandum principem sempiternum). The mass then proceeds, with appropriate prayers; the post-communion prayer must have been derived from a service book of the Carolingian empire, with its conscious revival of Roman imperial tradition:

O God, who for the preaching of the gospel of the king eternal hath prepared the empire of the Romans: extend to our king thy servant the heavenly arms, that the peace of thy church be disturbed by no tempest of wars.

At the end the bishop celebrant prays that the king may be stronger than all his enemies, and a rubric states that it is righteous that a king newly elected and raised upon his throne should enjoin these three commandments on the Christian people subject to him:

First, that the church of God and the whole Christian people should keep true peace at all times.

Another thing: that he should completely forbid rapacity and all crimes to all ranks of people.

A third thing: that in all judgments he should enjoin justice and mercy, that to him and to us the clement and merciful God should show forth his mercy.

Many forms of blessing follow in the pontifical, and then prayers and offices for Ash Wednesday, Palm Sunday, forms of absolution for penitents, the blessing of holy oil for the sick, and the chrism, and prayers for the Maundy, holy Saturday and Easter. A long series of episcopal[1] blessings for the various feasts and saints' days follows, including those of St. Germanus and St. Martin, St. Judoc, St. Anthony, and St. Erkonwald, the common of a martyr, many martyrs, a confessor, many confessors, a virgin, many virgins; a blessing given at the time of a synod, and another 'blessing to be said over a king at the time of a synod'.

Among the miscellaneous prayers and blessings at the end comes the prayer at the ordeal of hot iron (the ordeal at the time was administered in church): God is entreated by the invocation of his holy name to make plain a just judgment, all falsehood being removed; and two forms follow for the blessing of the iron by the bishop, who anoints the iron with holy oil and prays that God who preserved the three children unharmed in the furnace of the Chaldees will preserve the innocent unharmed from the touch of the iron and make manifest the guilty.

The coronation rite used by Dunstan in 973 was a rich rite, with features both of political and sacerdotal interest. The bishops, abbots and lay magnates assembled for the festivity: the lay magnates and people awaited the king in church, and the bishops and abbots accompanied the king in procession: he entered as part of a great ecclesiastical procession. The old 'mandatum regis' appears in the rite for the first time as a 'promissio regis': instead of commanding that the peace be kept, etc., the king (as the Carolingian kings did) makes the threefold promise to the people: he demands also that

[1] These blessings, pronounced by the bishop at mass, varied according to the day; they originated in the Gallican rite, where they preceded the communion. They were adopted into the Gregorian sacramentary where they associated with the Pax. In France and England, when a bishop celebrated, he used one of these blessings instead of the 'Pax domini sit semper vobiscum'. The deacon, in one continental form, proclaimed 'Kneel down for the blessing' to a standing congregation (Humiliate vos ad benedictionem): the bishop then gave the blessing.

they promise allegiance (or the old hold oath) to him: as it were, in return for the promise he makes to them. This all comes at the beginning, not the end, of the service.

Then follows his investiture with the regalia, the sword and ring introduced for the first time, and by Frankish example. It is still not laid down that the clergy shall present the royal symbols, though it soon became their exclusive privilege. Then follows the anointing and blessing of the king by the bishops, and the cry of 'Vivat rex' is turned into an anthem sung by a choir of clergy.

Some of the Germanic inauguration ceremonies are relegated to the coronation banquet. Of Edgar's banquet we have an account by a monk of Ramsey, written c. 1000: the king sat on his bench in the hall and beside him the archbishops of Canterbury and York. The guests sit about them and the harper[1] sings his glory. The queen meanwhile has her own banquet in a room near by, where she has assembled the abbots and abbesses; the ordo for her own investiture and coronation has followed closely the Frankish rite.

Not directly connected with Edgar's coronation, and yet allied to it as part of the coronation ceremonial on the Continent, is the famous scene when the six (or eight) northern kings rowed Edgar on the Dee, the king himself taking the helm; such service was comparable with the service of the German princes at a coronation banquet.

The Anglo-Saxon royal anointing and coronation was a rite borrowed in its most important particulars from France: but the fine ordo composed by Dunstan, with its imaging of the king as a half sacerdotal person, had in its turn wide influence in western Europe. Abbot Fulrad of Saint-Vaast, near Arras, was a friend of Dunstan, and c. 980 there was drawn up, in his abbey, a coronation rite, based partly on the Anglo-Saxon ordo, and partly on the west Frankish ordo: this 'Fulrad ordo' came to Corbie soon after its composition and about 1100 was adopted in place of the west Frankish ordo as the normal rite for the coronation of French kings; it was also used in the kingdom of Jerusalem. While the old Byzantine emperors ruled the church as the descendants of Constantine, west European kings ruled the church in their lands by virtue of an anointing the church itself had conferred. In England, the crown-wearings of the

---

[1] Scald: skald, a Norse word. The Norsemen settled in York called its streets by Norse names: to a monk of Ramsey, near Peterborough, the Norse 'skald' might come more naturally than the age-old 'scop'.

king were not merely a splendid pageant, but could only come after clerical coronation. The chronicler known as the Anonymous of York insisted that the king received the same anointing with chrism as the bishops, and even that he could therefore save souls and absolve sinners; perhaps in perception of the danger of such a doctrine, the royal anointing after 1066 was given with holy oil, but not with the more honourable chrism. The legend of Edward the Confessor's healing of the scrofulous woman appears to be connected with his power as anointed, and a similar power of healing was attributed to the anointed kings of France. In fact, the belief may go to pre-Christian magical powers attributed to the king: but such an origin was long forgotten.

The authorship of the great Christian hymns and poems used in the liturgy tends to be anonymous: and no great monument of liturgical verse can be ascribed to the monastic followers of Dunstan and Æthelwold. Yet they used the manuscripts sent to them from Frankish abbeys, and used the chant, the tropes, the sequences as Fleury, Saint-Denis, Corbie, Mont-Blandin and the rest used them.

Three fine pieces of Latin verse, their translations still familiar today, may be mentioned as used by the monks of the tenth century reform, and probably also by the clerks of the smaller minsters, in the last age of the English church before the Conquest: one a hymn, one a sequence, one an antiphon.

The famous *Veni, Creator Spiritus*, sung at the consecration of English kings and bishops, and before the lifting and translation of relics, is by tradition ascribed to Raban Maur, the pupil of Alcuin and great scholar abbot of Germany.[1] He died in 856: and though his authorship of the hymn is uncertain (he was not a great poet), the hymn was ninth century and must have been brought by the Carolingian renaissance to England; it was earlier than Byrhtferth of Ramsey's hymn, *Come holy Ghost* (see p. 64).

It runs:

veni, creator spiritus,	accende lumen sensibus,
mentes tuorum visita,	infunde amorem cordibus,
imple superna gratia	infirma nostri corporis
quae tu creasti, pectora.	virtute firmans perpeti.

[1] See Deanesly, M., *A history of early medieval Europe*, 1960, 510-512, and Raby, F. J. E., *A history of Christian Latin poetry*, 1953, 179.

qui paraclitus diceris	hostem repellas longius,
dextrae dei altissimi,	pacemque dones protinus,
fons vivus, ignis, caritas	ductore sic te praevio
et spiritalis unctio.	vitemus omne noxium.
tu septiformis munere	per te sciamus, da, patrem,
dextrae dei tu digitus,	noscamus atque filium,
tu rite promisso patris,	te utriusque spiritum
sermone ditans guttura.	credamus omni tempore.

As to the use of the sequence in England: the music and forms of the Gallican books, or the Eighth century Gelasian[1] with the Alcuinian supplement, must have been followed before the tenth century reform. There is no evidence as to what music the English monks sang at the mattins of Easter Day, when, according to the *Regularis Concordia*, the three brethren went, as it were, searching for Christ's body (pedetemptim) to the sepulchre; but in memory of this search, and the finding of the angel, and his message of the Resurrection, they must have prolonged the iubilus of the Alleluia at mass, and sung some form of the sequence. The Gallican form of the Alleluia and its verse had, up till the eighth century, followed the Ambrosian form, with its melody prolonging each verse of the psalm; but Gregory I had ordered that the music of the iubilus should be brought into closer relation with the words. Notker, the scholasticus of Saint-Gall, had had a book of sequences in the older manner brought to him by a monk who fled from his abbey of Jumièges when it was wrecked by the Danes, and such sequences must have been used in England: but Notker wrote sequences in the Roman manner, with one note to a syllable: and Latin verses with such syllabic music began to come into use.

The Easter sequence with the syllabic chant recounts, as it were, the search at the sepulchre of Easter mattins. The structure is that which Notker used at Saint-Gall,[2] not, that is, with verses having a set number of lines, and lines with a set number of syllables, such as Boniface's scholarly nun friend, Lioba, had sent him in Germany, but with verses of two, three or four lines, a rhythm dependent on the stress accent, and occasional rhyme at the line endings. It seems to have been written before 1050 by an imperial chaplain away in Germany, and the little tune to which it was sung had one note to a

---

[1] See chapter VI.   [2] See Raby, *op. cit.*, 217.

syllable, in the manner of the church at Rome. Those who sing the sequence to the traditional syllabic melody today may reflect that they are carrying out the musical prescriptions of pope Gregory I. The sequence runs:

victimae paschali laudes
immolent Christiani.

agnus redemit oves,
Christus innocens patri
reconciliavit
peccatores.

mors et vita duello
conflixere mirando,
dux vitae mortuus
regnat vivus.

angelicos testes
sudarium et vestes
surrexit Christus spes mea
praecedit suos in Galilaea.

credendum est magis
Mariae veraci
quam Iudaeorum turbae fallaci.

scimus Christum surrexisse
a mortuis vere,
tu nobis victor rex, miserere!

dic nobis Maria
quid vidisti in via?
sepulchrum Christi viventis
et gloriam resurgentis.

One of the liturgical books most commonly found in Old English wills and inventories was the troper (troparium), and it is evidence of the liturgical singing of trope and antiphon in the great English churches, as in the Carolingian abbeys; though, again, no English authorship can be claimed for any particular piece. A trope, with its musical accompaniment, came into use in the liturgy as introduction, addition, or sung comment upon a scriptural text already in use: tropes were written for the Introits, Kyrie's, Graduals, Gloria, etc. Tropes like the *Viri Galilei* for the Ascension, the *Hodie cantandus est* for Christmas and many other feasts, and other tropes, were already sung in the German abbeys, notably Saint-Gall; an Easter trope,

quem quaeritis in sepulchro
o christicolae?

comes from a manuscript of Saint-Martial of Limoges of c. 933–936.[1] The dramatic dialogue of the Easter mattins as recorded in the *Regularis Concordia* was, in fact, a trope, a terse meditation in music on a passage of scripture.

[1] Raby, *op. cit.*, 221.

The 'antiphons', also at the date written out in the troper, now signified commonly the verses sung at the beginning and end of a psalm, or set of psalms. They supplied colour and interpretation to the psalm; psalms were selected for singing at particular feasts not so much for their general content, as for some particular verses long associated with the history of redemption, or with some category of saints. Thus the eighteenth (nineteenth) psalm: *Caeli enarrant gloriam dei*, was sung at Christmas under the antiphon of its verse: 'Tamquam sponsus Dominus procedens de thalamo suo', and on every apostle's day under that other verse: 'In omnem terram exivit sonus eorum: et in fines orbis terrae verba eorum'. The colour of the psalm changed with the antiphon. Psalm two could be sung at Good Friday mattins under the antiphon: 'Astiterunt reges terrae, et principes convenerunt in unum: adversum Dominum et adversum Christum eius', or at Christmas mattins under that other verse: 'Dominus dixit ad me: Filius meus es tu, ego hodie genui te'. Antiphons had been in use long before the tenth century: St. Benedict wrote of the singing of 'six psalms with their antiphons', and Cassian of 'singing three antiphons, standing'. The year-long and repeated singing of psalms had no monotony for the monk who sang them as coloured by the antiphon under which they were sung.

The antiphons to the psalms were now supplemented by others sung with versicle, respond and collect, for some particular intention (as, for instance, in England, for the king and royal family). The antiphons at the end of vespers, compline, or other office, implored with particular beauty and solemnity the help of our Lady, full of mild-heartedness to sinners and the helpless. The beautiful antiphon,

> Alma redemptoris mater, quae pervia caeli
> porta manes et stella maris . . .

was already sung after compline during Advent and Christmas: it is ascribed to the crippled monk, Hermann of Reichenau, who died in 1054. From Le Puy in France came the later and more romantic *Salve Regina*,[1] expressing the longing in a rough and brutal age for a divine compassion, without measure and beyond reason:

> Salve, regina, mater misericordiae,
> vita, dulcedo et spes nostra, salve!

[1] *Ib.* 227.

ad te clamamus, exsules filii Evae,
ad te suspiramus gementes et flentes
in hac lacrimarum valle.
eia ergo, advocata nostra,
illos tuos misericordes oculos ad nos converte
et Iesum, benedictum fructum ventris tui,
nobis post hoc exsilium ostende,
o clemens, o pia,
o dulcis Maria.

The Carolingian renaissance in the ninth and tenth centuries had produced not only new liturgical forms, but a revived classical style in the illumination of manuscripts, in sculpture, and in the metal work of chalices, reliquaries, etc. In illumination, the Caroline illuminators used mainly Byzantine models, which were at hand in Italy, and their work is usually considered in schools, though these cannot be sharply marked off from one another. The earliest, the so-called Aix group, all belong to the age of Charlemagne: their evangelists' portraits are without symbols, as was usual in Byzantine illumination. The manuscripts of the so-called Ada group show some Celtic influence: but the figures are more humanistic, the composition rather heavy, and the colour very rich. The school of Tours and that of Reims used more nervous, linear drawing, with many small pictured scenes woven into the initials and between the lines of the text, and lively, almost agitated, figure rendering. In the mid ninth century a new school of illumination developed round the court of the emperor, Charles the Bald, and focussed in the scriptorium of Saint-Denis. In the tenth century, in the abbeys of the Ottonian emperors and the west Frankish kings, the figures showed greater delicacy of modelling and even more movement: drapery became more fluttering, and sometimes the manuscripts had lively sketches of both Christian and pagan episodes: Biblical personages and their anti-types in classical paganism.

In England too a new style of illumination developed, and after a particularly sharp break with the brilliant traditions of the Northumbrian and Hibernian schools. The Danish invasions completely interrupted the old traditions; a few outstandingly precious manuscripts were saved, but the illuminators and their monastic workshops were gone. The old Northumbrian painting had been decorative and non-representational; the new art sought to represent figures and scenes, even figures in movement, the emotion on their faces and the fluttering of their draperies. While inspiration came from Carolingian France and Germany, and even the Byzantine models these followed, English art developed on its own lines and had its own distinctive character. Something of the old Northumbrian influence survived in plait-work and interlace, something characteristic of the English spring and summer in the abundant, springing leafage, something in the English treatment of royal personages in a lighter and more human way than among the Franks. The Byzantine concept of the emperor had been largely accepted by the followers of Charlemagne and reproduced in the heavy majesty of their representation of Frankish emperors and kings; in illuminations the figures of English kings remained lively human people, sometimes in action. While rather grandiose figure compositions were popular in Carolingian art, with the emperor himself occupying the principal place, in the finest English manuscripts interpretation of a religious subject in a delicate and imaginative manner marks the peak of achievement.[1]

The first signs of the new approach to manuscript art after the Danish invasions appears in the illuminated initials of manuscripts written from Alfred's reign onwards, where full-page illustrations were not yet attempted. Most initials were made up of leaves and animal patterns, only a few having figures: but they were no longer in the tradition of abstract ornament. Full page illuminations only appear in the later days of Dunstan and Æthelwold: decorative initials occur in manuscripts of the reign of Alfred. The ninth century book of Cerne has full pages in the old Northumbrian manner, but its initials have endings in dragons' heads which became common in the post-Alfredian period, though the work in the Cerne book is heavier.

A manuscript of Alfred's *Pastoral Care*, written between 890 and 899, had decorative initials in thin line, with twirling animals' or serpents' heads painted in various colours. Other, tenth century, manuscripts have initials not only with dragons' heads, but with springing leaves, and even vegetation based on the Carolingian acanthus, lightly coloured. As the tenth century advanced, coloured initials replaced the earlier ones in line, and the treatment was stiffer

[1] For the whole subject of English illumination, sculpture and architecture, see Rice, D. Talbot, *English Art 871–1100*, 1952; for illumination, pp. 173–225.

7

and heavier: a mid tenth century manuscript of the *Heliand* (Saviour), with rather stiff drawing and muddy colouring, was certainly written and illuminated in the west of England, probably at Glastonbury. In the third quarter of the tenth century the linear initials with a few primary colours gave way to a more ornate type of letter closely allied to the full page illuminations: it has been suggested that the stiff rods and sprouting leaf work of these initials suggested the characteristic 'frames' of full page illuminations of the 'Winchester school'. The history of initials and pages of decoration is henceforth closely allied: the matter of colouring and the drawing form part of a universal style, in use from about 960 onwards. Though it had earlier antecedents on the Continent, it reached its full development at the hands of English artists.

Though the new style of decoration has become known generally as that of the Winchester school, not all the examples came from Winchester. Some were indeed produced in the Old and New Minsters, like the Arundel MS.60 psalter, with its full page, bordered Crucifixion, from the cathedral: and the famous *Liber Vitae* (see p. 134) from the New Minster:[1] but other refounded monasteries produced beautiful work of the same school: Medehamstede and Ramsey, Glastonbury and Abingdon and Canterbury. While the Carolingian illuminations developed under strong classical influence and the desire to reproduce the civilised Roman past, with indeed few fine examples of Germanic or Celtic art to look back to, in England there was a mixed tradition. The old, glittering pages of abstract art[2] were not reproduced: but in the work of some monasteries elements of barbaric art were still to be found among the leafage and naturalism of the humanist design. In such illuminations as the evangelists' portraits of the York Gospels (late tenth century), the evangelist still sits in timeless space within his fixed frame, though his posture is life-like and his drapery flutters; but in other evangelist pages, the fixed frame has become the abundant, leafy, Winchester 'frame': no barrier between time and eternity. The Winchester school combined with outstanding success the old barbaric and the new classical ornament, and it inspired all the English illuminators.

[1] Rice, 217 ff.
[2] See Kendrick, T. D., *Late Saxon and Viking art*, 1949, 1-22, and Wormald, F., *The Benedictional of Æthelwold*, 1959.

The revival of classicism was not, indeed, completely new: the newest art critics find more of the classical and less of the insular traditions in such works of art as the Bewcastle cross and the Lindisfarne gospels. But to the court of Alfred, who spent most of his life fighting the pagan northmen, the humanistic, Carolingian art seemed essentially Christian, and the heavily stylized figures and animals of the older decoration less Christian because barbaric. Church ornament became more classical. Queen Ælflæd ordered a stole and maniple to be embroidered for bishop Frithestan of Winchester (909–931), and they embroidered for her figures and scenes in the Frankish manner; king Athelstan later presented the stole and maniple to St. Cuthbert, as he lay in his shrine at Chester-le-Street, and they are popularly known as St. Cuthbert's, though made long after his day. King Athelstan firmly desired to obtain the help of the saints, and to this end he was a great collector and donor of relics, and also a donor of other precious objects; besides the Winchester vestments he bestowed on the shrine of St. Cuthbert a copy of Bede's life of St. Cuthbert. This has a fine full page picture of Athelstan offering the book to St. Cuthbert: within a 'frame' a crowned king stands under an arch, and holds an open book towards the saint, in chasuble and alb, standing before a church with tiled roof, clerestory and aisles. The illumination was painted in 935: the elaborate scroll work of the frame, and the classical figures of king and saint, are heavily coloured and clumsy compared to later Winchester work; they are a not very good imitation of Frankish painting.

The manuscript whose illumination a note ascribes to Dunstan himself is a continental treatise on grammar, and the title page shows a large figure of Christ seated, holding in one hand a rod and in the other an inscribed panel, with a tiny figure of the monk Dunstan prostrate at his feet. The picture is an artistic composition executed in line drawing: the drapery flutters, and Dunstan hides his eyes in his hands. There is no 'frame', and the manuscript may be Glastonbury work of c. 950.

The full beauty of the Winchester style is seen in the illumination of the charter by which king Edgar made his gifts to the New Minster, and in those of the Benedictional of Æthelwold. In the charter, within a foliated 'frame', king Edgar holds aloft the charter and gazes up to Christ, sitting enthroned within a mandorla (pointed oval frame). On either side of the king stand the blessed Virgin and St. Peter, while above four floating angels support the mandorla. The drapery swings: the angels are in motion, and the king, standing with his back to the spectator and facing Christ, swings his head round that his face may be seen. The frame, no longer the old Greco-Roman device that took the figure out of this world of motion and struggle into a timeless and serene world of its own, has now become a decoration; its foliate leaves almost move, and the figures within step or fly in front of it as the artist pleases. The picture within is no longer still and timeless; the figures move and the drapery flutters with human breezes.

The Benedictional of St. Æthelwold belongs to the same period and style, that of the 'Ada' and 'Metz' period among Frankish illuminators, where the figures drawn are somewhat coarse and stolid, and the faces stare blankly; when movement is shown in the drapery and composition but not yet in the figures. The Benedictional was written at Æthelwold's order between 975 and 980. The most splendid page has St. Æthelthryth within a foliated frame of acanthus leaves set between the double bars of the rectangle and the circles of its corners: the saint is veiled, haloed, and holds a flowering branch: within the frame is written 'Imago sancte Ætheldrythe', as in the earlier portraits of evangelists with 'Imago sancti Iohannis', etc. Imago in the manuscripts is always a pictured image. In the illumination of Christ's baptism, Christ in a mandorla stands deep in a wavy, rushing river: floating angels hold draperies to veil his body, or perhaps, hold his garments, and the dove rushes swiftly down head first from heaven, as in the oldest representations. In another richly illuminated page St. Benedict stands before a curtain which, in the old mosaics, indicated that he had passed from this world: he sits on a chair beneath an arch, holding his rule, and within the splendid frame are drawn the turreted walls of his monasterium. The composition is closely comparable with the old evangelist portraits of the insular school.

In all these illuminations, and in those of the Winchester style in general, the colouring is exceedingly rich, and much gold is used. An effect of gorgeousness is achieved by copious and blended use of pink, blue, purple and green: the illumination gives the impression of a colour design of great richness. The design itself is no longer abstract, as with some of the pages of the old Hiberno-

Saxon school, but a naturalistic figure, or a scene, within a gorgeous frame.

The tenth century reform was marked also by a wave of church building, very insufficiently represented by the churches that have survived. For this there are two reasons: the frequent use of timber, and the habit of rebuilding churches in important places.

First, as to the plentiful use of timber as building material, either by itself, or in conjunction with stone: early stone churches were only built where there was good limestone, as from the limestone ridge running down the centre of northern England, and in the Cotswolds; southern and eastern England were poor in stone, and timber building prevailed. Such buildings were not only more perishable than stone ones, but more apt to be cleared away as old-fashioned, and replaced with stone. There are a few literary references to such replacements: Æthelric, bishop of Durham (1042–1056), pulled down a wooden church at Chester-le-Street and built a stone one for St. Cuthbert;[1] Wilton and Lewes had wooden churches, similarly replaced. Some wooden churches, like that surviving at Greenstead in Essex, had walls of split tree trunks, set upright and touching: Greenstead had a rectangular nave, and its small chancel has only recently been excavated. Essex was not a good county for building stone. It had not, indeed, many trees with tall, straight trunks, such as are needed for stave work; the relative scarcity of such timber in England probably accounts for the greater use of half-timbering, or frame work. The evidence that such work was extensively used comes from the frequent reproduction of timber structural details in stone churches: though whether the timber-influenced style developed first on the Continent and was copied here, or was used here independently, is uncertain. Pilaster strips such as appear as decoration on the late tenth century towers of Earls Barton and Barton-on-Humber are imitations in stone of the frame of a timber building. Often, however, pilaster strips in England were functional and not merely ornamental: they hold together the rough work of the walling. The use of flat impost blocks and form of many Saxon mouldings also points to earlier models in timber.

It is clear also that right down to the Conquest wood was

[1] Rice, 52.

frequently used in the upper storeys of towers, and this not only from manuscript illustration, but from the surviving stone supports for such towers. They would not have been strong enough to support stone towers. The towers of Saint-Riquier, Saint-Wandrille, Cologne, etc., had such wooden upper storeys; the churches of Chichester and Selsey had wooden towers.

Stone supports have also been found for wooden galleries at the west end, and for wooden staircases within stone or wooden turrets. Where such evidence remains, it shows that literary accounts of lofty towers and churches built on an elaborate plan were not exaggerated. The coronation churches where English kings were crowned at Kingston-on-Thames and Bath have not survived; they were timber churches. But it is unlikely that they were mean or unworthy buildings, as they were chosen for such solemn rites: Kingston-on-Thames had been the scene for royal anointings from Alfred to Edgar.

The second reason why the tenth and eleventh century churches are but poorly represented by their survivors is that the large and important churches were in important places, and cleared away in the ardours of Norman rebuilding. Only the small churches, on relatively unimportant sites, have survived: but it is not on the obscure and the second-rate that the achievement of the age should be judged. Certain surviving features in altered churches (like the first floor Saxon doorways surviving unapproached in the wall), and the stone supports of timber structures in churches much altered, give credence to literary descriptions of elaborate churches which have not survived at all. That of Wilfrid at Hexham has been mentioned by Eddius; that built at York by archbishop Æthelberht or Albert about 780 was even more elaborate. Alcuin, in a poem, described it as very lofty and supported on columns, as 'sparkling with panelled ceilings and shining windows, with many surrounding porticus; many upper chambers it had with varied roofing, and thirty altars variously adorned'. Albert had built his great church because fire had destroyed its predecessor: and of Albert's church, which must have had galleries and circular staircases, nothing remains. Little remains either of the great tenth century churches; most were destroyed by the Normans, or altered out of recognition.

As to the Continental models that inspired visiting English ecclesiastics in the tenth century and filled them with the desire to have churches like them, in some measure, in their own country: they were derived from the Mediterranean, Byzantine world, the Mediterranean civilisation that spread from Visigothic Spain to Asia Minor, and had trading connexions with Persia and even the Far East. The textiles of Persia and such things as ivories and reliquaries, at least, were brought camelback to Trebizond and Byzantium, and show their influence on the ecclesiastical ornament of the west. But as regards architecture, the influence of the east as shown in the dome, and centrally planned buildings, had been established much earlier. Byzantine influence, however, was still operative among the Carolingian Franks, and through them, on England.

It helped produce the style known as 'Ottonian Romanesque' among the east Franks, where the tenth century churches had a great variety of ground plan, ovals, trefoils, octagons and, for very large churches, three aisled basilicas with an apsidal termination to the west as well as the east. The east end of large churches had usually a large transept, and the west end also a transept: both might have towers over the crossing of transept and nave. The west end sometimes had a gallery with an altar in it. The nave had no transverse arches or vaulted roof.

The tower developed as a decorative feature in these east German churches: not as a place of sanctuary under attack, like the stone round towers of Ireland, or as bell towers like the separate plain bell towers of Italy. The Ottonian towers were square in plan, usually built with each storey slightly smaller than the one beneath, and decorated with open arcading. The churches had also smaller, round, towers, with circular staircases: English churches too in the ninth and early tenth centuries began to be built with them. The larger churches in Ottonian Romanesque began to have ambulatories round the main apse, and chapels for minor saints radiating from apse or ambulatory. The habit of pilgrimage consequent on devotion to the saints brought Englishmen to France and Ottonian Germany, and spread knowledge of the new churches and decorations. Oswald knew Fleury and Dunstan knew Ghent and the churches they must have passed on their travels; Oswald built a great new church at Worcester and made considerable land grants to two separate 'artifices'; and 'artifex' must have been the architect or master mason of his church (see p. 150); it is possible that the architect also had seen Continental churches, or else been content to work to

Oswald's own design. On the whole, English builders in the early tenth century looked to Germany: in the late tenth century, to France.

The influence of Ottonian Romanesque can be seen in tenth and early eleventh century English churches, and especially in the accentuation of the architectural importance of the west end. A western apse or sanctuary is not as commonly found as in Germany, but it was used in certain cases. Christ Church, Canterbury, had at the time a western as well as an eastern apse. The use of a western gallery was common, all over the country, and sometimes it had an altar in it. Deerhurst had such a gallery and altar; Barnack had a central niche and two side niches in the western wall, and the ground floor of the western tower of Barton-on-Humber, square in plan, may have been used as a western chapel. The central tower, its upper storey of wood, now began to be built under German influence: whereas earlier the common plan of the English church had been one of two chambers, nave and chancel, with a quite narrow arch between (or, in the south, a triple arcade): now churches of three chambers were built, aligned or roughly aligned; nave, central section under the tower bounded to the east and west by arches, and the chancel. Double splayed windows also came from the Rhineland.

Perhaps the most influential model among the western Franks was the great church of Saint-Riquier near the mouth of the Somme. This had a double transept, at east and west ends, with a staged tower at the two crossings of the nave and round staircase towers at the corners of the transepts; a single apse at the east end contained the main altar, and the walls were decorated with scenes from the New Testament in relief or stucco. An early example of such a church in England was that built by St. Swithun for the Old Minster before his death in 862; his church was much altered by Æthelwold. Rather later churches, Frankish or Ottonian in character, were archbishop Oda's church at Christ Church, Canterbury; Æthelwold's churches at Winchester, Oswald's at Worcester and the new church for St. Cuthbert at Durham (999). Great abbey churches were built at Ely (c. 1000); Ramsey (970); Thorney (972); Dunstan's church at Glastonbury, and the surviving abbey churches at Peterborough (of 970 or earlier) and Elmham (of c. 1000).

From the monk Eadmer's description, we know that Christ Church immediately before the Conquest had a semicircular eastern apse, and also a western one in the German manner; it had a lofty crypt, probably for the relics. Æthelwold's church at the Old Minster had a large atrium, a number of chapels and (from the picture in Æthelwold's Benedictional) a great, five-storeyed tower. The church at Durham had two towers of stone, one at the west end and one over the choir, probably at the crossing. Oswald's new church at Worcester, dedicated to St. Mary, covered much ground; when it was damaged by the Danes, the remains had to be cleared away by Wulfstan II before he could erect a new church. Ramsey had two towers, one over the crossing, and Thorney altars at both ends, like the double-ended German churches; Glastonbury had a tower, as well as a crypt. Peterborough had a transept, with a small presbytery projecting from it. The church at Elmham, of which much remains, had a long nave, a T-shaped transept at the east end with a semicircular apse projecting from the centre, a large square tower at the west end and smaller ones in the angles between the transept and nave. Most of the important churches thus had a T-shaped transept and many had a central tower supported on arches: the space beneath separated the chancel from the nave. The inner surfaces of surviving walls are often of rough work, and may have been covered originally with painted plaster, or relief work.

As to the smaller churches, served perhaps by a single priest, or the two or three clerics of a small minster:[1] nearly 200 churches survive, either Saxon or Saxon with Norman additions.[2] Many had upper storeys, galleries or chambers in the tower, and the usual means of access to such upper floors was by means of wooden staircases and ladders.[3] The high side doorways at such churches as St. Paul's, Jarrow, Tredington (Worcs.) and Wing (Bucks.) must have given access to western galleries. Four surviving churches have stone staircases, and other great churches must have had them. Many churches had towers with upper storeys of wood, and, no doubt, belfry windows; of the stone belfries that remain, most have double windows, but single windows were also used, and, occasionally, double windows on two sides, and single windows in the other two walls, as at Bardsey (Yorks.). Barnack in Northamptonshire had four

[1] Such small minsters were still found, and are evidenced by several entries in Domesday. [2] Rice, 64.
[3] See for the results of modern research on these late Saxon churches, Mr. H. M. Hope Taylor's 'Some Aspects of English pre-Conquest churches', in *The Anglo-Saxons*, ed. P. Clemoes, 1959: for turret stairways, p. 152.

triangular openings near the top of the Saxon part of the tower. Though these Saxon towers were not very tall, and sometimes had upper storeys added by the Normans, they were yet in proportion to the original small church. The villager at the period must have been familiar with such a church, lofty in his eyes, and familiar also with the summons of the church bell.

Among the smaller, surviving tenth century churches, Deerhurst stands out, as the church of a moderate sized, a non-royal, minster in the Cotswolds, a minster with its own large parish. It was an old foundation, possibly made by a Mercian king, and Heming, the monk of Worcester who compiled the famous Worcester cartulary, states that there was a minster at Deerhurst soon after 804. It was ravaged by the Danes but survived as a minster of clerics, and was joined by the young Ælfheah, later archbishop of Canterbury. Deerhurst lay in the sphere of Oswald, bishop of Worcester's activities, and was refounded as a Benedictine house c. 970; whether Ælfheah was still there is uncertain. The new abbey had a fine church, but it was on the borders of Mercia, whose earl Ælfric led the anti-monastic reaction. It found a defender later in earl Odda of the Hwiccas, the champion of monks and enemy of the Godwine's. He rebuilt or enlarged the church at Deerhurst, received the monastic habit there, and died there in 1056.

The church as rebuilt in the refoundation of king Edgar's reign (c. 970) had a long, narrow nave, an eastern apsidal, polygonal chancel, and two porticus at the eastern end, making the church cruciform. Above the crossing of nave and porticus was a central tower, and at the west end a gallery with an altar; a long porticus prolonged the western end of the nave. To support the tower, a wall was built across the western end of the nave, pierced by a narrow arch; the space under the tower was perhaps used by the monks' choir. Before the Conquest, and perhaps by the efforts of Odda, four new porticus were added in the angles between the nave and transepts and chancel and transepts.

The surviving ornament at Deerhurst illustrates the character of the church throughout its pre-Conquest history. Its stone font, dating from c. 910, belongs to the period when it was a clerical minster, having the care of a parochia. Like all Saxon fonts, it is large: large enough for the priest to immerse the naked baby, holding his right hand over the baby's nose and mouth, before delivering it to the godparent to wrap in the chrisom cloth; the font is supported on a carved block of stone, to make it a convenient height. Its ornament is in the old tradition of spirals and interlaces that survived in places right down to the Conquest: the double spiral on the outside of the font is remarkable. Also early, belonging to a period of rebuilding in the tenth century, is a stone angel, the work of a carver following probably a manuscript illumination for the wings, and the style of hairdressing; the original influence is Byzantine, and the wide open, staring eyes suggest the Ada period of Carolingian illuminators. A stone Virgin built into the eastern wall of the west tower at Deerhurst has the holy child standing before the Virgin's knees, and belongs to the period c. 1000; it has a curiously flattened, unfinished appearance, and some shading may have been indicated by paint; the Byzantine type followed may have been copied from a lead seal, for which the type was sometimes used.

Comparable in size to Deerhurst were the churches of Stow (Lincs.), of c. 1000–1016, with transepts and handsome transeptal arches at the crossing; St. Mary at Dover, with its two axial towers; Repton, with its early crypt and columns and vaulting of c. 1000, and the fine churches of St. Bene't's, Cambridge, Earls Barton and Sompting,[1] with its pyramidal tiled roof set above a four gabled square, a reminiscence of Carolingian and Ottonian Germany. Of the centrally planned churches of the Continent, however, no English example has survived; though, curiously enough, there is reason to believe Alfred, with his memories of Rome, had such a church built at Athelney. Asser says it had four columns in the centre, and was built after his own design; also that the churches Alfred built were 'more venerable and precious' than the works of his predecessors.

Of all the late Saxon churches showing Carolingian influence, the church abbot Wulfric had built for St. Augustine's, Canterbury, is the most remarkable. Though he could not make the whole church centrally planned, for it consisted of the original basilica finished under Lawrence, and the smaller, aisle-less church of St. Mary built to the east on the same axial line, he yet joined them by a centrally planned octagon crowned by a roof higher than the earlier structures and possibly domed. Wulfric was abbot from 1047–1059; he had been to Rome, and perhaps seen the centrally planned St. Costanza.

[1] The towers only of St. Bene't's and Sompting are still standing.

He had passed through Dijon, where the church of Saint-Bénigne resembles in many respects his own new building, and had been itself built between 1011 and 1018. Wulfric had the east end of the original basilica of SS. Peter and Paul pulled down and the west end of the church of St. Mary opposite to it: the arched openings that replaced the walls became two sides of the new octagon, whose inner wall was actually circular. The north and south sides of the octagon were buttressed by semicircular towers, projecting like apses. There is no evidence however that the new octagon contained an altar.

As to the adornment of these late Saxon churches: the metalwork of reliquaries and church furniture remain and show that they were remarkable; and so, in their own day, must have been the more perishable wood carvings, textiles and church paintings. All the fine objects were the work of individual craftsmen, but inasmuch as they copied or were inspired by Continental illuminations and models, their work conforms to the contemporary enthusiasms and schools. The delicate draperies of the Carolingian illuminators appear in the ivories of the Virgin and Child, the leaden seals and the stone sculpture. The repertory of ornament in Britain was similar to that in northern Europe, and in many respects to that of Italy and the Mediterranean countries.

Among the few examples of sculpture that can be mentioned are the pair of flying angels at Bradford-on-Avon, of c. 950: they were part of a large rood carving, and bear veils on their arms in the Byzantine manner. They are really drawings in stone, silhouetted figures enriched with simple engraving, and very near to the manuscript illumination on which they were modelled.[1] Byzantine ivories seem frequently to have been the models for English sculptors, as in a bust of Christ at Gloucester, and the figure of Christ in Bristol cathedral. Paintings and carvings of the crucifixion must have been fairly frequent, judging from survivals, most having the figure of Christ in a long, semi-monastic robe, like the Langford rood of c. 1020, or the crucifixion of Daglingworth, where the Christ wears a close-fitting tunic and the face has moustaches in the northern manner: or with a bare figure with the loin-cloth, as in the Romsey

[1] See for these angels, and other late Old English sculpture, Kendrick, T. D., *Late Saxon and Viking Art*, 1949.

rood of c. 1010.[1] The stone carving of the raising of Lazarus and the greeting of Christ by Mary and Martha at the gate of Jerusalem may date from c. 1080, but are purely Anglo-Saxon in concept and workmanship; they were cut up and transported to Chichester, perhaps from the older see-church at Selsey. The stiff folds of the drapery are Byzantine in character: the movement of the figures and emotion of the faces all in the style of the Winchester school of illumination.

No high crosses as splendid as those of Bewcastle or Ruthwell survive from this period, but the setting up of carved stone crosses was common throughout the period especially in the north. Some would have consecrated the burial place of a notable person: some appear to have marked a preaching station originally, and, when the church was built, to have remained in the churchyard, or even been incorporated into the church. Few whole crosses remain from this period, but many shafts carved with the old interlaces, the newer styles brought by the northmen, or with figure work.

The old Northumbrian traditions show in the panelled cross in Leeds parish church, with its single stiff, majestic figure to a panel; but in the many later cross shafts, the Carolingian-modelled versions of such crosses have figures in the panel more numerous and part of a decorative pattern. The cross shaft from Halton (Lancs.) has Christian figure subjects that have become mere surface decoration: it has also two panels with the purely pagan figure subject of Sigurd forging his sword, Fafni the dragon, Regni the Smith, and Sigurd toasting the dragon's heart.[2] While it is true that pagan practices still flourished in Yorkshire, to judge by the warnings in the Northumbrian Priests' Law, it seems that the juxtaposition of Christian and pagan subjects on a Christian monument (the Halton cross is not the only example) does not express any wish to compromise the Christian tradition, but rather that to the sculptor artistic interest was important rather than dogma. No offence was given to Christians apparently by the intrusion of these old fairy tales (for such they had now become) on a Christian monument. Similarly, the old poem of Beowulf had earlier been written down by a Christian poet for a Christian audience.

Among the sculptured crosses of the period may be noted the round cross shafts of northern Mercia. Many are found in the Peak district, but others of the type as far distant as Yetminster in Dorset

---

[1] Kendrick, *op. cit.*, 49.   [2] *Ib.* 59.

and Gosforth in Cumberland. The Gosforth cross is round at base, then tapers in four sides to the peak, where an equal-armed cross in circle, much carved, still survives; the subjects give equal importance to pagan myth (perhaps those of the Norse Edda) and the Christian gospel: most of the designs come straight out of pagan art. In Danish Mercia and East Anglia the crosses were set up, not with round, but with rectangular and panelled shafts; most were carved with the old interlace, or combination of interlace and figure; one, the cross shaft of Shelford (Notts.), has a stiff, barbaric rendering of a Byzantine angel on one panel, and an equally stiff, flat rendering of the Virgin and Child on the other.

Grave slabs and cross shafts, distributed throughout England, also show direct Scandinavian influence by their reproduction of the Jellinge, Ringerike and Urnes style. A grave cover at Levisham (Yorks.) has the Jellinge 'Great Beast', with its double outline and flat, ribbon-like body: a fragment of cross shaft at Kirkby Stephen, Westmorland, in the flat, exuberant Jellinge style, has a figure of the devil, bound, a ribbon ornament threaded, through rings, round his arms, his legs and his body.

Many carvings in the Ringerike style come from the southern counties, where lands were given to Danes by Æthelred in the hope that they would fight future invaders of their own race, and by Cnut, as a reward for service in the past. One such stone has the inscription in runic lettering: 'Kona caused to erect this stone to Tuki': Tuki, one of Cnut's followers, died in 1035.[1] The finest surviving Ringerike stone in this country is the gravestone of another servant of Cnut, like his master, converted to Christianity, but reared in the Scandinavian tradition: on this headstone, found in St. Paul's churchyard, the fight between the Great Beast and his enemy the Dragon is carved with the traditional spirals for limb-joints and flat, ribbon-like enrichments of the Ringerike style. It is art that came to Europe with the Scythian nomads, passed up the trade route of the great Russian rivers to the Baltic and Scandinavia, and flourished among the Viking stone carvers. As to the fight between the lion and the serpent, which belongs to Norse mythology, it appears here in a splendid design by itself; but Saxon sculptors found it attractive as a motif, as they have long liked dragons with open mouths and slashing tails, and in some cases they now represented the fight

[1] Rice, 128.

between St. Michael and the dragon with the ribbon ornament and spiral joints of the Ringerike and Urnes style. The carved tympanum over a church doorway at Southwell (c. 1030) has a figure of St. Michael brandishing a sword like a Norse Viking, and a scaly dragon whose body intertwines itself with a ribbon, foliated ornament that may represent its hind legs but looks much more like the old Ringerike serpent that fought the Great Beast.

Of all the pieces of church furniture mentioned in Anglo-Saxon wills, and so frequently that there is no doubt most churches had them, decorated and of rich material or simple and of some poorer material, there are comparatively few remains. Bishops had croziers, sometimes all of wood, sometimes with heads of ivory or metal: a beautifully chased metal head, crook-shaped, survives from Clonmacnoise, and an ivory one, a small, contorted figure with the crook, from Aghaboe: the beautiful ivory head of a tau-cross, where a small Saxon draped figure holds together the scroll work of the crozier head, much as a similar figure the scroll work of an initial in an illuminated psalter. The figures and designs on vellum are repeated in those worked in metal as well as in stone. Bells, rings, weather vanes, bowls, cruets, all had such patterns, as doubtless had the altar hangings (mæsse-reaf) and chasubles (mæsse-hacele): but for these, survival could scarcely be hoped for. In minster and village church, the open-eyed Christian, monk or priest, villager or his child, moved in a European world: the Celtic influence had retreated, a Scandinavian and near pagan one moved in: but the Englishman had dealt with all these art forms himself. His art owed most to the Franks, but it was now English, not merely Carolingian.

CHAPTER VII

THE LATE OLD ENGLISH CHURCH:
BISHOPS AND PASTORAL CARE

THE history of the Old English church between the days of Dunstan and the Norman Conquest is one of renascent piety and pastoral reform, and that though Danish raiding and eventual conquest destroyed churches, dispersed libraries and brought violent death to ealdormen and even bishops. The Danish king Swein attacked and conquered England before his death in 1014, and Cnut his son ruled England as king from 1015 to 1036. Harold, son of Cnut and Ælfgifu of Northampton, ruled England from 1037 with the help of earl Godwine till 1040: and during these years earl Godwine was responsible for the murder of young Alfred the Ætheling. Harthacnut, the legitimate son of Swein, was king from 1040 till his death in 1042; and Edward the Confessor, the murdered Alfred's brother, succeeded in 1043.

The general appointment of monks to be bishops in the period was safeguarded by the royal permission that monks should elect their abbot, according to the rule of St. Benedict, in the *Regularis Concordia*. Canon law already provided for the election of bishops by the episcopal familia, or the 'sanior vel melior pars' of it, and the Benedictine rule also for a choice by the 'sanior vel melior pars', if desired. The *Regularis Concordia* had in addition laid down that the monks should elect on the advice and with the choice of the king; and, in fact, such royal guidance must have directed most episcopal elections, even though a Benedictine chapter went through the motions of election. This is indicated by the frequent appointment of a monk from another house to be abbot bishop, for monks by themselves were not inclined to choose a monk from another house to be their abbot. That the monastic right to elect was actually given, at least in one case and probably in others, is shown by the authentic charter in which king Æthelred in 993 confirmed the earlier grants of Eadwy and Edgar to Æthelwold's monastery of

Abingdon. In any case, the reformers' pupils and successors got elected.

Yet in spite of wars and violence, bishops kept watch over clergy and laymen, held synods and issued rules for church people either through the king in witan, or in ecclesiastical synod. The people had little enough protection in these dangerous days from king or ealdorman, and sought it from the saints: the veneration of their relics was a popular movement, not imposed from above, and not to be separated from veneration of the saints themselves, as ready helpers of the poor and afflicted. The sustaining of faith and maintenance of Christian life among these disturbed people was mainly due to the appointment of pious and competent bishops, nearly all of them monks trained in a reformed monastery.[1] The first generation of the new type of bishop belonged to the immediate circle of Dunstan, Æthelwold and Oswald: their successors to the abbeys they had refounded or reformed.

At Canterbury, for instance, Dunstan's four immediate successors were all monks. Archbishop Æthelgar had been first a Glastonbury monk, then a pupil of Æthelwold at Winchester, who made him abbot of the New Minster at its reform, then bishop of Selsey and, in 988, archbishop of Canterbury.

On his death in 990 Sigeric, monk of Glastonbury and bishop of Ramsbury from 985, succeeded: Ælfric the homilist dedicated the *Catholic Homilies* to him.

In 995 he was succeeded by archbishop Ælfric, who had been a friend of Æthelwold and monk of Abingdon: the earliest life of Dunstan was dedicated to him.

In 1005 he was succeeded by Ælfheah, who had been a monk in Odda's minster of Deerhurst (see p. 98), then monk and abbot of Bath. Dunstan secured his appointment as bishop of Winchester in succession to Æthelwold in 984, and he was translated to Canterbury in 1005. He was captured by the Danish host in a raid on Canterbury in 1011, and taken on board ship and kept a prisoner until the time that they martyred him, in 1012.

Similar appointments of monk bishops were made in very many

---

[1] This has been shown in Professor R. R. Darlington's classical article, *Ecclesiastical reform in the Late Old English Period*, EHR. li (1936), 385-428; and see John, E., in 'Some Latin charters of the tenth century reformation in England', *Revue Bénédictine*, lxx (1960), 333-359; for the Abingdon charter of 993, *ib.* 337 and KCD. no. 684.

other sees. At York, Æthelwold's pupil Ealdwulf succeeded Oswald in 995: he had been bishop of Worcester since 992, and held the two sees together. Before that, in 963 he had been set over the monks of the newly restored house of Medehamstede, and had, as the Peterborough chronicle says, enriched it with many lands. Æthelwold's influence also secured the promotion of his pupil Ælfstan of Abingdon to the see of Ramsbury, which he held from 970 to 981. Dunstan's monks and monastic friends also received bishoprics: Ælfwold of Glastonbury went to Crediton (998–c. 1008), Brihthelm of Glastonbury to Wells in 956, Cyneward and Sigegar from the same house to Wells in 974 and 975 respectively. Ælfwine, abbot of Westminster when it had been reformed by Dunstan, went to the see of Wells in 997. The see of Elmham was held by bishops associated with Dunstan from 1001–c. 1021; as was that of Winchester by Æthelwold the Younger, 1006 to c. 1012 (he had been prior of Glastonbury and abbot of Abingdon).

The Old Minster of Winchester trained a great number of monks who became bishops: besides Ælfheah, Sigegar and Ælfstan, mentioned already, there were Sideman of Crediton, Eadnoth of Dorchester, Æthelsige of Sherborne, Wulfgar of Ramsbury, Ælfstan of Rochester, Ælfheah of Lichfield, Æscwig of Dorchester and Athulf of Hereford.[1]

All these bishops were personally known to Dunstan, Æthelwold and Oswald and appointed before c. 981; but after the death of the three great leaders the tradition of appointing bishops from reformed monasteries was maintained. In Cnut's reign, the archbishopric of Canterbury was held by Lyfing, who had been prior of Æthelwold's reformed monastery of Chertsey, then bishop of Wells in 999, then archbishop in 1013. Æthelnoth, who succeeded him in 1020, had been a monk at Glastonbury, then dean of Canterbury (see p. 157): he was Cnut's chief ecclesiastical adviser throughout his reign. Other monk bishops included Eadnoth, Æthelric and Eadnoth II of Dorchester (1006–1049 altogether); Ælfward of London (1035–1044); Ælfmær of Sherborne (1017–1023); Lyfing of Crediton (1027–1046); Ealdred of Worcester (1046–1062); Brihtwy (called Merewit) of Wells (1027–1033); Brihtwold of Ramsbury (c. 1005–1045); Æthelwine of Wells (1013–?1027); Leofsige of Worcester (1016–

[1] For these reforming bishops and the sources mentioning them, see Prof. Darlington's article, supra.

1033) and Brihteah, nephew of archbishop Wulfstan, at Worcester (1033–1038); Æthelric, the last English bishop of Selsey (1058–1070), a Canterbury monk and very learned in the traditions of that church; Siward of Chertsey, about 1085, a monk and provost of the cathedral monastery there. He greatly admired the traditions of St. Oswald and the reforming bishops, and was honoured for the piety of his life and the ability of his rule even by the Norman prelates after the Conquest.

There are few adverse comments on these monk bishops from contemporary chroniclers, and many of them were stated to have been men of sanctity: Wulfstan of Worcester (1062–1095) was canonised: archbishop Æthelnoth of Canterbury and Eadnoth of Dorchester were both termed 'the Good' by contemporaries, and Æthelstan of Hereford was described as 'a man of great holiness'. Others are described as strict and ascetic: maintaining, that is, the traditions of St. Æthelwold. Ealdred, who held the sees of York and Worcester, was a good monk reformer, and tried to relieve the poverty of the see of York from his own property: he bought lands with his wealth (how, as a monk, he could still command family property is not clear), and gave them to endow his churches of York, Southwell and Beverley. That the English bishops were not yet regarded as feudal potentates, maintaining and leading their own armies, is shown by the disapproval expressed of Leofgar, bishop of Hereford, who fought in battle, after great provocation. In 1055 the Welsh prince Gruffydd had joined the outlawed earl Ælfgar and raided and burned the town of Hereford, where Leofgar's predecessor, the aged Æthelstan, was bishop; they sacked the famous minster, stripped it of its relics and vestments, and slew the priests within: Æthelstan died soon after and Leofgar succeeded him. A writ of 1056 says of Leofgar that 'he abandoned his holy oil and his cross and his spiritual weapons and took up spear and sword and went thus on an expedition against Gruffydd and was slain there and his priests with him and Ælfnoth the sheriff and many other good men'.

In the reigns of the Danish kings and Edward the Confessor certain foreigners were made bishops, but usually as coming from reforming monasteries, notably those of Lorraine. The two Lotharingians, Giso of Wells (1061–1088) and Leofric of Exeter (1050–1072; see p. 76), were accepted as good and generous bishops, strict canons by training, but not regarded as differing greatly, in a cosmopolitan age, from the English Benedictines. The unpopularity of Normans appointed by Edward the Confessor, as, for instance, Robert of Jumièges, was due to suspicion of political motive rather than evidence of bad life.

Of accusations of simony made by Norman chroniclers against the Old English bishops, most seem confused and ill-founded. The long practised holding of York and Worcester together was due to the poverty of York rather than the simoniac appointment of a succession of greedy prelates; Lyfing of Crediton held the see of Worcester in plurality for seven years altogether, but the see of Crediton was very poor. Ramsbury was another very poor see, and when Herman was appointed bishop in 1045, he tried to take over the wealthy monastery of Malmesbury as his episcopal see and failed; after an interval as monk of Saint-Bertin in Flanders, he returned and was allowed to hold the sees of Ramsbury and Sherborne in plurality. The difficulty of running a see with quite insufficient endowment is illustrated by the failures to subdivide some of the sees of Wessex, the new, small sees all collapsing through lack of funds.[1]

In the reigns of Cnut and the Confessor, however, not all the bishops appointed were Benedictine monks: some received sees as rewards for long and good service in the royal writing office, now well organised and trained for the writing of vernacular writs and use of the pendant royal seal.[2] The royal scriptorium was not yet called the chancery, for there was no chancellor: by definition, a 'cancellarius' was a notary, trained in Roman law, and the English laws being insular there was strictly no need of a chief notary or cancellarius. Yet the scriptorium-trained bishops of Cnut's and Edward's reign were the predecessors of the most frequent type of

---

[1] The division of the see of Winchester into two at the accession of Frithestan in 909 was apparently part of a reorganisation scheme connected with pope Formosus (see Darlington, supra, 105 n.): the scheme envisaged five new sees for Wessex, Sherborne being divided at Asser's death in 909 into three small sees, Wells, Sherborne and Crediton. King Athelstan added a see for Cornwall at St. Germans or St. Petrocs (Bodmin). All these sees proved financially viable. But a see of 'Berkshire', of which Cynesige was described as bishop, and a cathedral establishment at Sonning (Wilts.) both collapsed. Efforts to subdivide the see of Winchester before the arrangement of 909 had all failed, probably for financial reasons: it is possible that the names of one or two unknown bishops who attested ninth century charters were *chorepiscopi* working in Wessex.

[2] See ASW., 11-19.

Norman bishop: the clerks trained in the chancery. Of the pre-Conquest bishops trained in the royal writing office the outstandingly bad example was Stigand, for whose plural holding of the sees of Winchester and Canterbury no good reason or excuse can be alleged. He had been a royal clerk or chaplain to Cnut and Harold Harefoot, and adviser to Cnut's widow, Ælfgifu-Emma; he received the see of Selsey in 1038, his brother Æthelmær that of Elmham; in 1047 he received the see of Winchester, and supported earl Godwine; when Robert of Jumièges was driven from the see of Canterbury against king Edward's will, Stigand's friends were strong enough to insist on his receiving it, though it was not canonically vacant. Stigand used Robert's pallium at Canterbury, for he did not receive one of his own; he is said to have held several abbeys (certainly that of Gloucester) in plurality, and he retained the see of Winchester while in possession of Canterbury. He was papally excommunicate, and bishops avoided receiving consecration from him: nor was he asked by his friend, earl Harold, to consecrate the new abbey of Waltham which he had founded. The notoriety of Stigand's misdoings supplied an excuse to the Normans to decry the state of the English church.

As to the maintenance of Benedictine monasteries to serve cathedral churches, according to the policy of Æthelwold and Oswald, there is nothing to show that the next generation had less faith in this policy. At Christ Church, Canterbury, where Dunstan had been content to continue the régime of strict clerks living the 'vita canonica', archbishop Ælfric introduced Benedictine monks, apparently between the years 995 and 1006. Wulfsige of Sherborne transformed the familia of his cathedral from a secular to a monastic one c. 992, and monks may have been introduced at Crediton at about this time. King Æthelred made generous grants to monks, and so did the Danish king Cnut and his wife, Ælfgifu-Emma. Edward the Confessor allowed his 'man' Urk and his widow to bequeath land to the monastery at Abbotsbury which Urk had founded, and was otherwise generous to Benedictine houses throughout his reign, crowning his policy by the magnificent refoundation of Westminster abbey;[1] he granted a hundred court with the profits

[1] See ASW., 286-295, for criticism of the surviving sources in which Edward confirmed and increased the landed estates of Westminster.

of jurisdiction to Abingdon, confirmed rights to Christ Church and St. Augustine's, and made grants to Ely, Ramsey, Winchester, Chertsey, Coventry and other houses.

The continued preference for a familia of Benedictines rather than strict canons to serve a cathedral church would seem to have been connected with the fear, so great in England, of the diversion of the landed endowments from the church. Sons of the cathedral clergy might seek to inherit their fathers' prebends, which could not happen with a Benedictine chapter; fear of the influence of noble relatives of strict or secular canons was still great. There was a danger of diversion even with Benedictine houses; it was held greater in the case of houses of canons. Although the indubitable sign of true monastic life was, in the tenth century, considered to be the communal holding of landed property, some charter evidence suggests that an abbot or bishop might grant land with the consent of the community to his own relations or thegns, and even apart from the common practice by which abbot and community leased lands for one or three lives for the community's benefit; and even these long leases seem to have been equivalent to a benefaction, for there was difficulty about reclaiming them at the end of three lives.[1] Oswald granted land for a similar term to 'my thegn, Ælfric': but this may have been payment for doing fyrd service for abbey lands, or some secular obligation. Oswald, again, leased land at Hindlip in 996, with the consent of the community, to his kinswoman Ælfhild and two heirs: after their death to revert to the foundation at Worcester for the use of the bishop.[2] The priest Æthelnoth granted an estate to the New Minster with all the lands king Edmund had given him, 'with the right of giving it to strangers or kinsmen with all the freedom which king Edmund has given me', king Eadred and two bishops being witness.[3] The difficulty of reclaiming lands held under a long lease is illustrated by the terms of a grant made by bishop Brihthelm of Winchester, enjoining in the name of God and St. Peter that no one should be so presumptuous as to keep it longer from the church.

It is possible, that is, that in spite of all the reformers' insistence on the communal holding of minster property, there was still a danger that bishop or abbot might seek to benefit relatives or thegns from

---

[1] Or even a grant for one life: 'after Ketel's death, the estate is to go to St. Edmund's without controversy', ASWills. no. 33. Cf. KCD. no. 464, for a grant, where it is stipulated that on the grantee's death, 'nullus eligatur haeres'.
[2] ASChar. no. 42.   [3] Ib. no. 28.

grants or leases of monastic property: that the old danger of family patronage of minster lands was well remembered in England: and that the Benedictine rule was held a surer safeguard of communal holding than the rule of strict canons.[1] And that though a Benedictine familia was less obviously adapted for the training of the diocesan clergy than a canonical one: and provided no archdeacon or 'high deacon', an officer the tenth and eleventh century Anglo-Saxon bishop was beginning to value. Reverence for the English tenth century reformers remained great, and sustained the Benedictine abbeys which served bishops' sees: though such service was very infrequent on the Continent.

There are, of course, no episcopal registers, much less parish archives, for this period of the late Old English church, so that the best evidence for the pastoral care of her bishops is that of the holding of synods and passing of canons, or the holding of witans with attendant bishops and the passing of laws dealing with church matters. This kind of evidence is plentiful; if the bishops in England had no notaries, the tradition that the 'acta' of a synod should be notarially transcribed had been passed down and even applied to those of the witan; the bishops had well-educated clergy in their familia able to make quasi-notarial records. 'Synodus' was a word that meant 'meeting', and in the pre-Conquest period was still not used exclusively of a meeting of bishops or clergy, which renders the distinction between the king's witan and an episcopal assembly more difficult.[2]

It is clear that a body which passed secular and ecclesiastical laws should be termed a witan; but when only ecclesiastical clauses were enacted, in the king's presence and by his authority, it is less easy to give the assembly a name. The original record would almost certainly

---

[1] It is not likely that the bishop's involvement in apparently military matters had any bearing on the question. Whether the bishop had a familia of monks or canons, he would probably be responsible for the fyrd service some of his lands might owe to the king: the thegns to whom he had granted leases would perform it. References in charters more often refer to ship service than to fyrd service: bishops apparently bequeathed to the king a ship as well as coats of mail as a kind of heriot. Bishop Ælfwold of Crediton (997–1012) left the king a 64-oared ship (EHD. 536), and archbishop Ælfric (1005–1012) also a ship (EHD. 544).

[2] Wilkins, Conc. i. 294, has a long footnote dealing with the question whether the witan at Enham was a witan or a synod, and the difficulty in general of deciding whether any particular 'synodus' was a synod or witan. The Enham meeting, he notes, was certainly a witan; but its character must be viewed against the general practice of promulging canonical codes in the witan.

have had a preamble stating the place, and perhaps the occasion, when the assembly was held: but many preambles have not survived: indeed, in the surviving manuscripts which have large compilations of Anglo-Saxon laws or canons, the preamble stating where, when and how the legislation was passed is usually lacking, and there are few cases of decisive evidence as to who drafted the legislation. Nor is there decisive evidence as to whether ecclesiastical laws were published in any exclusively episcopal meeting before the witan, or after. The general canonical practice on the Continent was for the archbishop to draft and publish his canons in a provincial synod and a bishop to draft and publish his canons in a diocesan synod.

There is very little evidence of discussion[1] or objections raised at any ecclesiastical synod (see p. 128), with the exception of the opposition at the synod of Chelsea, nor is there evidence of discussion or objection raised by the ealdormen or thegns to the king's secular laws in the witan; the king's bishop or clerk drafted them and the witan heard them; the difficulty was not their acceptance, but to get them carried out. Against this general background, it seems not unlikely that an archbishop, frequently Wulfstan in his lifetime, drafted the ecclesiastical clauses of a royal code, and that the assembled bishops heard them for the first time in the witan, and emphatically accepted them; it is possible that Wulfstan drafted the secular clauses also, or in conjunction with the king's writing-office, whose members were all clergy.

In any case, the bishops heard and should make a copy of the laws passed in the witan: but they had no reason to suppose such laws (canons) would become known to their own diocesan clergy unless they published them, or their own shortened version of them, in their own diocesan synod. Very little evidence as to the diocesan synods held has survived: but some has, together with directions that diocesan synods should be held.

The best evidence that ecclesiastical laws published under royal sanction in the witan were actually drafted by an archbishop, possibly after publication in an assembly of bishops beforehand, are the

---

[1] There was plenty of business to be transacted at synods, i.e. connected with the making of episcopal land sales or grants, or grievances raised by members of the synods, which other members were enjoined to treat as their own (see p. 131): the synod was not a silent assembly. But evidence of discussion about canons promulged is lacking.

opening and final notes of the Latin paraphrase of the laws passed at the council at Enham, which (translated) run:

These are the constitutions (a notarial word) which the English counsellors (members of the witan) chose and promulged, and insistently taught should be observed. This is the first ruling (consilium) of the council of bishops, that we should all turn most diligently from our sins.... (The text of the laws of Enham follows, both those of the first part which deal with ecclesiastical matters, and the second which deal with secular offences and military defence: matters outside the scope of canonical legislation, though the whole set of laws ecclesiastical and secular might have been drafted for the king before the council by Wulfstan. The paraphrase ends:)

These are the lawful statutes and decrees magnificently given and published (edicta) by king Æthelred in our synodal assembly (conventu synodali) and all the magnates of that time faithfully promised to observe them: therefore I, Wulfstan, by the Lord's grace archbishop of York, have written them out (literis infixi) for the memory of those to come and the salvation of men present and future: inspired as I am by the love of God and my neighbour. (The note suggests that Wulfstan made the record after the council: but study of Wulfstan's Anglo-Saxon homilies and the Anglo-Saxon version of the laws suggests that he, in fact, drafted the laws beforehand.[1])

Whatever the manner of drafting or publishing, the code of Enham, and a large proportion of Anglo-Saxon laws published in the witan at the period, express the pastoral care of the bishops.

With regard to ecclesiastical legislation passed in the witan, usually transcribed first in any code and followed by the secular clauses, but also appearing in some cases as isolated clauses among secular laws, there is one pointer to ecclesiastical drafting. This is the phrase: 'Docemus': in the Anglo-Saxon version, 'We lærath'. It occurs

[1] For the Latin paraphrase, see Wilkins, *Conc.* i. 286, 292, 294. More than one version of the Latin paraphrase has survived: and the Anglo-Saxon Codes V Æthelred and VI Æthelred seem to be either variant records of the same meeting, or re-enactments in nearly the same words at a later meeting: for these Codes, see Robertson, *Laws*, 78 and 90: and for a discussion of the whole matter of the relation of synod to witan, Professor Darlington in EHR. li (1936), 415-417. While it is certain that laws passed in the witan at this time were published and recorded in Anglo-Saxon, it is doubtful whether the formal record of canons drafted in a purely episcopal assembly, a 'synod' in the modern sense, would not have been in Latin.

frequently in the clauses passed by the witan at Enham: We biddath and lærath: in the Latin version in the same manuscript: Rogamus et docemus;[1] it is laid down that bishops shall diligently teach all their people, 'læran georne', 'diligenter docere',[2] and again, the bishop-drafted phrase, 'And we lærath swythe geornlice',[3] 'Docemus etiam instantius', and in other places in these witan-promulged canons. The phrase occurs frequently, both before and after the record of the witan at Enham: but never as enjoining a secular law. Even in the code II Cnut, where the preamble runs: 'This is the worldly ordinance that I will . . . that men hold all over England', the only clause beginning 'we lærath thæt' continues: 'even if any-one sins and commits grievous crime';[4] while the clauses for secular measures begin with the royal 'I will', 'Ic wylle', or 'We bid', or 'forbid';[5] or a clause is drafted 'If a man', 'If a reeve', do such and such a thing, then the appropriate penalty. In short: the king orders or forbids: the church teaches or exhorts.

The 'synodal laws', if one may call them such, promulged in the witan deal with miscellaneous matters: but each code shows what problems were particularly exercising the minds of the bishops at the time, and what measures particularly needed royal support. It is perhaps more illuminating to indicate the chief ecclesiastical enact-ments of each witan or code, taking them chronologically, rather than to analyse their contents and give a history of clerical celibacy, monastic irregularity, church dues, etc. (though for the last, see p. 118). The general picture built up by all the details of the king's and the bishops' laws is that of a church ruled from above by king and bishops, and not only ruled by the king but protected. Archbishops seek to get their reforms carried out by the king; his reeves help to enforce the payment of tithe, the rendering of the produce of every tenth acre traversed by the plough. Priests, the reforming bishops claim, know they should be celibate: but by old custom parish priests are regarded as lawfully married, and expect to pass on their church to a son in holy orders. A priest within his 'shrift-shire' must baptise babies, say mass in his church on Sundays and holy days and teach his people in English the meaning of the creed and Our Father; lay people must know these by heart.

---

[1] Wilkins, *Conc.* i. 286, and Robertson, *Laws*, 92.   [2] Wilkins, *ib.* 287.
[3] *Ib.* 287; and see VI Æthelred, Robertson, *Laws*, 90, 172, 174.
[4] Robertson, *Laws*, 174.   [5] *Ib.* 176.

Laymen must eschew violence and fighting, especially within the 'peace' of the local church, the 'church grith'. They must not be drunken or immoral or marry within the fourth degree. They must take no part in pagan rites, like well-worshipping or incantations round a tree or an earth-fast stone. They must keep oath and pledge and deal alms to the poor.

The code I EDMUND, quoting earlier laws and dealing only with ecclesiastical matters, enjoins that those in holy orders should observe the celibacy befitting their estate: this to apply to priests, monks and nuns; if they fail to do so, they shall incur the penalty 'that is quoted in the canon', forfeiting their worldly possessions and burial in consecrated ground. Tithes, church scot, Peter's pence and plough alms must be paid, on pain of excommunication. If any man shed a Christian man's blood, he shall not come anywhere near the king, without confession and penance (implies the denouncing of 'excommunication by infection', to be so important in the German court in the next century). Churches must be restored. Perjurers and sorcerers to be for ever cast out from the fellowship of God.

The code II EDMUND condemned those who committed secular offences to appropriate penalties, though the prologue stated that the king and witan have been considering how they could best promote 'Christianity': the offences to be punished are all violent offences: fighting, pursuing the old practice of the vendetta to punish murderers, instead of the king's law about compensation by payment of wergeld or manbot.

III EDMUND enjoined the swearing of an oath of allegiance to the king, further penalties against the pursuing of the vendetta, and those who harboured criminals; 'if a number of serfs (slaves) commit theft (cattle raiding), their leader shall be killed or hanged and each of the others scourged three times, have (part of) his scalp torn away and his little finger mutilated as a token of his guilt. (This harsh penalty is quoted as showing contemporary attitude to cruelty in a society where even the church tolerated the ordeal of hot iron or hot water: see p. 82.)

I EDGAR dealt with how men should hold the hundred court: ending 'The iron for the triple ordeal shall weigh three pounds'.

II EDGAR enjoined that God's churches should have all their prerogatives, and the manner of the payment of tithe (see p. 114), etc.: all the laws here issued by the witan dealt with ecclesiastical matters.

III EDGAR dealt with secular matters: the preamble says: 'This is the worldly ordinance (gerædnes) that I *will* that men hold'.

IV EDGAR said that king and witan believed that the widespread plague was due to men's non-payment of tithe, etc.: the king forbids (I and the archbishop forbid) men to withhold God's dues: secular matters and distinction between the practice of Englishmen and Danes come at the end of this long code (see also p. 119).

I ÆTHELRED (passed by the witan at Woodstock in Mercia) dealt with the maintenance of law and order by decreeing that every man have a surety responsible for him, who would swear to his character and innocence. (In a mainly village society, where there were of course no police, and the scientific examination of evidence was unknown, the trial of an accused man in the moot took the form of demanding that his surety, or sureties, the old oath helpers, should support his own oath that he was innocent (see p. 124). The graver the offence, the higher the rank, or the more numerous, were the sureties needed; if the accused could not find oath helpers, he went to the ordeal, single or triple according to the degree of suspicion in which he was held.) 'To go to the ordeal' was held in itself a penalty. Many of Æthelred's and later kings' laws dealt with the complicated structure of oath safeguards: the kind of oath demanded and the penalties in money for oath breach, for less grave offences where the ordeal was not demanded. The whole matter of perjury was a grave social and spiritual offence. The most frequent offence in the English village society, and the one most difficult to trace back to the offender or offenders, was that of cattle thieving: king Edgar had legislated about it, and this code of Æthelred sought to strengthen the law about sureties, partly to prevent the sale of stolen cattle.

II ÆTHELRED was a truce agreement made between king Æthelred, the Viking king Olaf and other Danish leaders: tribute should be paid them, to which archbishop Sigeric, ealdorman Æthelweard and ealdorman Ælfric agreed, and arrangements were made about breaches of the peace between Englishmen and Danes after the truce; if any Englishman killed a Dane, or vice versa, £25 compensation should be paid. None of these clauses was observed by the Danes nor any truce kept.

III ÆTHELRED dealt at length with breaches of the peace and false money (moneyers who work in a wood should be liable to the death penalty).

IV ÆTHELRED was also a lengthy code, dealing with tolls and the levy of customs in London. The actual gates of Aldersgate and Cripplegate were in charge of guards, and ships came sailing up to Billingsgate, and paid toll at the quay. The code shows that plenty of merchants from the Carolingian empire came to London: the men of Rouen with wine or fish: men from Flanders, Ponthieu, Normandy and the Isle de France round Paris: men from Huy, Liège, Nivelles and 'subjects of the emperor' (of the east Franks). Where merchandise went, books could and did go.

V ÆTHELRED had 35 clauses, of which the first 25 dealt with ecclesiastical offences, and were not prefixed by 'the king bids' or 'forbids'. The early clauses were general in scope: 'that we all love and honour one God', 'peace and goodwill shall be duly maintained'. Then comes: 'the king and his witan have made a law that innocent Christian men be not sold out of the land, least of all to the heathen', nor shall Christian men be condemned to death for too trivial offences: punishments shall be merciful, so that God's handywork, that he purchased for himself at a great price, be not destroyed. Moreover, the king and his witan have said that men of every estate of men shall do their duty according to their estate: above all, God's servants (theowas), bishops and abbots, monks and nuns and priests, shall live according to their rule. Every monk out of his monastery shall return to his monastery, remembering the vows he has made to God. The monk who has no monastery shall come to the bishop of his 'shrift shire', and vow to God and men to observe celibacy, the wearing of the monastic habit and the service of the Lord. Canons where their property admits of their having refectory and dormitory shall hold their minster with due order and celibacy, as their rule teaches; otherwise, it is right that he that will not do so shall forfeit the endowment (prebend). We enjoin (biddath and lærath) all priests to avoid the wrath of God: they know full well that they have no right to marry; he who is celibate shall have the wergeld and privileges of a thegn, but he that will not be celibate as befits his order shall have a less honourable spiritual and worldly status.

Moreover: Christian men shall avoid illicit unions: Christian churches shall have the protection of the king and all Christian people, and no man may oppress or sell a church or turn out the minister of a church without the bishop's consent. Ecclesiastical dues shall be promptly paid every year, plough-alms, tithe, Peter's pence, light payments (leohtescot) three times a year; it is best that 'soul-scot' (payment, apparently, for burial in the churchyard, with a requiem) should always be rendered before the grave is closed; such payment to be made to the minster to which the deceased belonged, even if the body be buried elsewhere than its 'right shrift scire'. (The old minsters normally had the parochia and graveyard, though thegns' rural churches might have been built within the old, large, minster parochia.) Feasts and fasts and Sundays shall be duly observed: St. Mary's feasts zealously honoured: St. Edward (the Martyr's feast kept on March 18. Widows shall live respectably, not marrying for a year, after which they shall do so if they choose. Every Christian man shall go frequently to confession and receive the sacrament and carefully abide by his oath and pledge; injustice shall be zealously cast out; untrue weights and false measures shall not be used, nor perjuries, murders (death workings), thefts, drunkenness, violations of holy orders and of marriage. And let us loyally support our one royal lord to whom we have sworn the 'hold oath'.

VI ÆTHELRED. This seems to be a variant form, or a re-enactment of the preceding code:[1] it is rather longer, and has some interesting clauses not found in V ÆTHELRED. Priests (as before) 'know full well that they have no right to marry': in addition: 'But some are guilty of a worse practice in having two or more wives, and others, although they forsake their former wives, afterwards take others while these are still alive, a thing which no Christian man ought to do (let alone a priest). This clause, in both codes, points to the existence of a considerable number of married secular priests: their married status cannot be justified by canon law: but it is worse when they live irregularly as no Christian should). An additional clause about the marriage of laymen adds that 'it must never happen that a Christian man marry among his own kin within six degrees of relationship or within the fourth generation (or 'knee')[2] or with the

---

[1] Cf. the texts in Robertson's *Laws*, 78–108.
[2] See 'The Canterbury Edition of the Answers of pope Gregory I to St. Augustine', in the JEH., x (1959), 9.

widow of a man as nearly related to him, or with a near relative of his first wife; nor must he marry a professed nun or his godmother or a divorced woman, and he shall never have more wives than one. As regards feasts and fasts, the keeping of the Ember Days is enjoined in addition.[']

It is accepted that archbishop Wulfstan drew up the codes in Æthelred's reign, and in that of Cnut. An old code, long known as the *Laws of king Edward the Elder and Guthrum*,[1] is now also accepted as having been drawn up by Wulfstan; and though it is not possible to date it, or assign it a place among Wulfstan's codes, it is much less detailed than the last two codes of Æthelred, and may well have been earlier. The code deals particularly with a country in which the Danes are strong, and may represent some kind of agreement with the northern Danes; the first clause lays down that all are to love one God and reject paganism; apostasy to paganism is to be punished. If any ordained person fight or commit fornication, he shall pay compensation according to his wergeld; if a priest instruct his people falsely about feasts or fasts, he shall pay 30 shillings among the English, among the Danes a mark and a half (£1. 0. 0.: priests among the Danes would be poorer than among the English). If any ordained person have done anything worthy of death, he is to be brought before the bishop for judgment. Penalties for incest follow. No guilty person is ever to be denied confession before execution. Then, penalties for withholding tithe: working on feast days or breaking fasts: ordeals and the taking of oaths are forbidden on feast days, with due penalty among the Danes and fine among the English; no one to be executed on Sunday, if possible. If a man be judged to lose a limb and it be cut off and on the third day he be still alive, help may be given him with the bishop's pardoning grace, if any man desire to heal his wounds and his soul. Those who make incantations, perjurers, poisoners or those polluted with public harlots shall be driven from their own region: and all such evil doing shall be rooted out in this region and unless it cease there shall be heavy fines.

VII ÆTHELRED (laws issued at Bath): a purely ecclesiastical code: surviving in a Latin and a shortened Anglo-Saxon version. It was enjoined by king and witan that God shall be loved and honoured, the king obeyed and the land defended. In view of special danger,

---

[1] Wilkins, *Conc.* i. 202-204.

special prayer and fasting was ordered: payment of a penny from every plough land, so that every man who has a familia (apparently, not a mere villager, but with a household of dependants: the thegn of a village who has an 'aula') shall see that each of his dependants give a penny, and if anyone is without money his lord shall give it for him: and every thegn shall give a tenth of all that he hath. Every adult Christian to fast on bread and water and herbs for three days, to go to church without gold or ornaments, to go to confession, and every priest walk barefoot in the procession (singing the litanies and carrying the relics) with his people on the three days: every priest to sing 30 masses, every deacon and clerk 30 psalms; serfs (slaves) to be exempt from work on the three days, so that they may fast the better, and they may work for themselves as they will. The money penalties for breaking the fast followed: from 30 pence for a poor freeman to 120 shillings for a thegn, and the money to be divided among the poor; the priest and reeve of every village to be witnesses that this fast and almsgiving be carried out and to swear to it on the relics.

In every religious house a mass 'Contra paganos' to be sung daily, and the whole community, after the various 'hours' of the office, are to lie prostrate on the ground and sing 'Lord, how are they multiplied that rise up against us?' and the collect, 'Contra paganos'.

All church dues ought to be rendered and no one shall deprive God of what belongs to him or our ancestors granted him: and we forbid that anyone shall be sold out of the country: may omnipotent God show mercy towards us and grant us victory over our foes and peace.

The whole code illustrates the pressing miseries of the Danish raids, and the urgent prayer needed for divine help. An Anglo-Saxon version of the same code (VII Æthelred) has a preamble stating that this edict was issued when the great (heathen) army came to this country: the three days' fast and litanies were enjoined for the Monday, Tuesday and Wednesday before Michaelmas.

VIII ÆTHELRED: enacted in 1014, by king and witan. It has several opening clauses guaranteeing protection (local peace: church 'grith'), with the penalties for slaying a man in a church breach of church grith): compensation must be paid to the church and to the king; so with other offences done in church, compensation must be paid both to the church and to the king.

Not all churches have the same status: the 'head minsters' (heafod-mynstres grithbryce) have a compensation (bot) that equals that payable for breach of the king's peace (mund); the minsters of middle rank, 120 shillings; the lesser ones (the lesser holy places), 60 shillings; field churches, 30 shillings. As to tithes, king and witan have agreed that it is just that a third part of the tithes should go to the repair of churches, another portion to the servants of God (monks or clergy), and the third portion to God's poor and to poverty-stricken slaves. Every Christian man to give the produce of the tenth acre traversed by the plough, under the penalty king Edgar instituted (see p. 115). The tithe of young livestock to be paid at Pentecost, that of the fruits of the earth by the equinox or at least by All Saints: all church dues shall have been rendered by Martin-mas. Regulations about the ordeal, for priests, deacons (see p. 115). If a priest commits homicide or other great offence, he shall be deprived of his ecclesiastical office and banished, and travel as far as a pilgrim as the pope appoints for him. A priest committing perjury, or acting as accessory to thieves, to be cast out from the fellowship of holy orders and lose every kind of privilege: and clear himself by the single or triple ordeal prescribed for laymen (hot water or hot iron); but if a priest orders his life as the book (canon book) teacheth, he shall be entitled to the wergeld and privileges of a thegn: let him understand that it is not seemly for him to have anything to do with marriage or with worldly strife.

We desire abbots and monks to live more according to their rule than they have been accustomed to do until now: the king bids all his reeves to support the abbots and to help their stewards every-where to obtain their rights, so that they themselves may remain secure in their minsters and live according to their rule. . . . For in the assemblies (gemotan) since the days of Edgar, though they have been held in famous places, Christ's laws have been neglected and the king's laws disregarded (i.e. the shire moot and the hundred moots have not enforced the laws made by Edgar). . . . Things have gone from bad to worse, both in God's business and the world's. . . . But let us do our duty and take as our example what the secular witan of old wisely decreed: Athelstan and Edmund and Edgar who came last: how they honoured God and kept his law. So let us loyally (holdlice) support our one kingly lord.

IX ÆTHELRED: the beginning only of a code made at Woodstock.

X ÆTHELRED: in the preamble, king Æthelred declares he has been considering how he can best promote Christianity (Christendom): what ordinances he shall make, religious and secular. This ordinance we wish shall be observed in accordance with our decree at Enham. (The scribe has copied only two clauses further.)

King Cnut made no change in the character of the laws, ecclesiastical and secular, of his predecessors in England. He issued however two proclamations (with no mention of the holding of a witan) and one long code, the first part dealing with ecclesiastical, the latter with secular matters: here the publishing of the code in a witan is mentioned.

I PROCLAMATION, 1020: in effect, a royal writ. Cnut sends friendly greetings to his archbishops, the people's bishops, and earl Thurkill and all his earls and common people. . . . I bear in mind the written and verbal advice that archbishop Lyfing has brought me from the pope: that I should upraise the glory of God and suppress injustice and keep good peace (frith). . . . I bid my archbishops and all my people's bishops that they uphold God's rights . . . and I bid my ealdormen to support the bishops. . . . If any man, whether one in orders or a layman, Dane or English, presumes to defy the law of God and my royal authority and will not desist, I bid earl Thurkill to bring the evildoer to justice; and I likewise bid my reeves, under pain of forfeiture, to govern justly and give right dooms by witness of the bishops of their (shrift) shires: and to inflict such mild penalties as their shire bishops may approve. . . . The whole nation, men in orders and laymen, to keep the law of Edgar. The bishops say that oath breach shall cost men dear with God, and men shall put away slayers of kin, murderers, perjurers, witches, adulterers and the incestuous: no man shall presume to marry a nun. We enjoin that Sundays be kept, with no trading or assembly: men shall attend church and keep fasts and saints' days. (In all these matters the Danish followers of the king, newly converted or unconverted, might have held themselves excused.)

II PROCLAMATION, 1027. Cnut, king of England, Denmark, Norway and part of Sweden, greets Æthelnoth the metropolitan (metropolitanus: the text is in Latin), Ælfric, archbishop of York and all the bishops and lords of the whole English race, nobles and commoners. I notify you that I have lately been to Rome, for the redemption of my sins and the safety of my kingdom (his journey has been a pilgrimage). I had long vowed this journey to God, but have not been able to perform it till now. Now I give thanks to God who has allowed me to visit his holy apostles Peter and Paul, and all the holy places of which I could learn, both within the city and without, and to worship and adore there in person.

My chief reason for so doing was that I have learned from the wise that blessed Peter the apostle received great power from the Lord to bind and to loose, and that he was the key bearer of the kingdom of heaven. For this reason particularly I thought it extremely useful to seek his patronage with God very diligently. . . . Now there was a great assembly of nobles there at the Paschal solemnity, with the lord pope John (John XIX) and the emperor Conrad and indeed the princes of all nations from Mount Garganus to the North Sea: and they all received me graciously and honoured me with gifts. (Pope John crowned Conrad emperor during Cnut's visit, on March 26, 1027.) They gave me golden and silver vases and mantles (pallia) and very precious vestments. (King Cnut then relates that he has remonstrated about the heavy tolls and customs his subjects have to pay on their journey to Rome: the emperor and king Rudolf agreed to do away with barriers and tolls in their case; the pope also agreed that Cnut's archbishops should not pay the usual heavy exactions when they went to fetch their pallium. All this was sworn to on oath, as witnessed by four archbishops and twenty bishops and very many princes and nobles: Cnut must have raised the matter in the synod held at Rome on April 26, 1027.)

King Cnut then states that in thanksgiving to God he has vowed to rule his people justly, and to amend whatever he has hitherto done wrongly; some more clauses follow about peace between English and Danes, the payment in England of the customary church dues, and the enforcement of such dues by Cnut's officials.

I CNUT and II CNUT. This appears to have been a long (single) code, the first part dealing with ecclesiastical, the second with secular matters; it was published in a witan held at Winchester at Christmas: the year is not stated in the preamble, but certain evidence suggests that it was issued after Cnut's return from Rome in 1027. It covers much ground, and would seem to contemporaries a fine, up to date, edition of 'the laws of king Edgar'; it may have been compiled and issued in fulfilment of Cnut's vow at Rome to rule his people justly and constrain his sheriffs and reeves to use no unjust force towards any man. The phraseology of these Anglo-Saxon laws is reminiscent of Wulfstan's compilations, especially the rhythmic, general comments (let each man advise himself how he will: rade swa hwæther swa man wille; let him understand who can: understande se the cunne; lose his life and his land: tholige landes and lifes; by sea or by land: sy hit on scypfyrde, sy hit on landfyrde; by word or by work: wordes and weorces).

I CNUT, after the preamble, begins the old guarantee that each church is rightly within Christ's special peace (grith: private peace), and such peace is to be respected most zealously: the peace of a church and of a Christian king must always remain inviolate: he who violates them shall lose land and life: compensation due for committing homicide within the walls of a church. . . . Not all churches have the same status in civil law (wordly worship): repetition of the old distinction between head minsters, medium minsters, smaller churches with a graveyard, and field churches. . . . Great and wonderful are the things a priest is able to do for his people, if he duly serve his Lord: great exorcising and wonderful hallowing when he baptises, and holy angels hover around there . . . and if it happen that an accusation . . . is brought against a priest who lives according to a rule (i.e. monk or canon), he shall say mass, if he dares, and clear himself by his own denial and receiving of the holy housel; if the accusation be triple, he shall clear himself if he dare with two oath helpers also in orders. (A deacon must thus clear himself of a single accusation with two oath helpers of his own ecclesiastical rank; for a triple accusation he shall need six oath helpers of the same ecclesiastical rank, himself being the seventh.) If an accusation be brought against a secular priest not living by rule (neither monk nor canon), he shall clear himself in the same way as a deacon living by rule; a friendless servant of the altar with no oath helpers shall go to the ordeal of receiving the holy housel and fare as God wills (see p. 116).

Then follow detailed directions about monks and clergy accused of pursuing the vendetta, being the accomplices of thieves, committing perjury or false witness; in general, 'he shall make amends as the bishop shall prescribe for him'. All the servants of God and priests above all must practise celibacy ('they know full well they have no right to marry': see p. 114). Christian men shall never marry within six degrees of kindred, or with the widow of a man as nearly related as that, or with a near relative of his first wife; nor shall he marry a professed nun or a repudiated wife . . . and he shall have no more wives than one and remain with her as long as she lives.

The payment of the various church dues and the penalties for non-payment are both restated in detail (see p. 115); in addition, it is allowed that a thegn with bookland who has a church and grave-yard may give a third of his tithes to his own church: the church dues from every household to go to the old minster (which would still have a large parochia or shrift-shire). The laws about feasts and fasts are reiterated (see p. 118), and about ordeals, confession, going to the holy housel at least three times a year, etc. It is newly enjoined (we lærath thæt) every Christian shall learn the Pater Noster and the creed: if he learn them not he cannot receive the holy housel or be given Christian burial or lawfully stand sponsor at a baptism or at a confirmation (the laying on of the bishop's hands): not until he learns it and knows it well.

The bishops are God's heralds (beadles) and teachers (lore servants) . . . let him who will take heed. The bishops are shepherds who must guard the people against spoilers, of whom the devil is chief: they must cry out against this ravening wolf.

II CNUT: 'This further the secular ordinance which I, with the counsel of my witan, will to be observed over all England' . . . 'This is then first, that I will right laws to be upheld and everything unlawful willingly suppressed.' (Some of these secular laws affect Christian conduct: Christians should not be condemned to death for light offences, or sold oversea; wizards, sorcerers and prostitutes shall be everywhere driven out, and also apostates: thieves and robbers shall be made an end of, unless they repent.)

We earnestly forbid all heathen practices, that is, the worship of idols, heathen gods, sun and moon, fire or flood, watersprings or stones or any of the trees of the wood: or the love of witchcraft, or death-working in any wise, either by sacrifice or divination or the practice of any such delusions.

The laws go on to reiterate directions about man-slayers, perjurers, those who injure the clergy and adulterers, robbers and plunderers;

about the currency, and false money, weights and measures; repair of forts, bridges, the preparation of ships; and all the dues owed to the king by the men of Wessex, and from the Mercians, and from the Danes, respectively, and in detail. Failure in oath or ordeal is next dealt with, the old savage penalties of having the hands or feet cut off, the eyes put out, part of the scalp removed, etc., specified. Slaves found guilty at the ordeal shall be branded on the first occasion, and be put to death on the second; he who swears a false oath on the relics and is convicted shall lose his hand, and half his wergeld, which shall be divided between the lord and the bishop.

The first 36 clauses of this code deal mainly with secular offences, though including the ecclesiastical matters mentioned; the remaining clauses, 37 to 84, deal mainly with lawful punishment or bot to be adjudged for them. There is an interesting reference to canon law as known to all: 'ecclesiastical amends shall be exacted in accordance with the (canonical) scriptures, worldly bots in accordance with worldly law'. The slaying of a servant of the altar can be amended by pilgrimage or the payment of compensation to his kin; many other clauses are merely repetitions of some law of king Æthelred; there are, however, new and detailed laws about the payment of heriots, or payments at death, in armour, horses and mancuses of gold to the king. It is also laid down that a wife must guard the keys of her storeroom, chest and cupboard: if stolen goods are found in them, she is held guilty; but she cannot prevent her husband depositing (stolen) goods in his cottage. . . . And may God almighty have mercy on us all, as his will may be.

In short, the laws of Cnut show no difference in character from those of king Æthelred or 'the incomparable Edgar'. There is no suggestion of condoning pagan practices by the Danes in the north, or those of Cnut's circle of leaders and bodyguards. Wulfstan drafted some of the early laws, and an ecclesiastic in his tradition the later ones. The tenth century reform and its principles were maintained.

Curiously enough, no record survives of any code of laws issued by Edward the Confessor in a witan, though there is plenty of reference to the holding of such royal councils. Edward had a well organised scriptorium of clerks, and his writs are of great interest;[1] if he had published a code, it is most probable that it would have

1 ASW., p. 18.

been recorded and survived. The law as it stood at the close of Cnut's reign was deemed sufficient: to secure its observance by the English partisans of earl Godwine, who inherited an older anticlericalism, was another matter.

The other instrument of episcopal care in the late Old English period, beside the issue of canons or quasi-canons by synod or witan, was the holding of diocesan synods for the priests, and the making of a diocesan visitation by a bishop to see that his directions were carried out. The chief evidence for the holding of such synods and visitations are three codes of laws for priests surviving in manuscript: dated references are lacking for the holding of particular diocesan synods or visitations (visitation of their sees once a year by all bishops was enjoined by archbishop Oda in Edmund's reign[1]). Beside the three codes for priests, there are one or two collections of English canonical literature, particularly a large compilation in Old English which Benjamin Thorpe in his *Ancient Laws and Institutes of England* surnamed *Institutes of Polity, civil and ecclesiastical*.[2] The collection is usually known as the *Polity*, though no such title is found in the manuscripts, but only the headings of sections: 'Of bishops': 'Of the church': 'Of the members of the witan', etc.

The duty of priests to attend the diocesan synods is laid down in the canons Ælfric the homilist wrote for bishop Wulfsige of Sherborne (?998).[3] It is headed: *Of the priests' synod*, opens with an exhortation to priestly celibacy supported with summaries of the teaching of the scripture on the subject, together with that of the synod of Nicaea (neither bishop, mass priest, deacon nor regular canon should have a woman in his house except his closest, specified, relation). Then comes a brief description of the seven clerical orders (monkhood and abbothood are in another order), and the obligation of priests and God's servants (theowum: monks) to sing the seven canonical hours. Priests before they are ordained shall have a psalter, epistle book, gospel book and mass book (mæsse-boc), manual, an

---

[1] Wilkins, *Conc.* i. 213; from a MS. with many canons, Vesp. A.14.

[2] Published 1834, p. 422 seqq. The 'Polity' is found in C.C.C. Camb. MS. 201, the great collection of Wulfstan's homilies, together with many O.E. codes; in Cotton MS. Nero A.I, a Worcester MS. with Wulfstan's *Sermo Lupi* and many codes; and in Bodl. MS. Junius 121: see *supra*, p. 56. The two first-mentioned MSS. have also the *Northumbrian Priests' Law*.

[3] Thorpe, *Anc. Laws*, i. 441-451. The Anglo-Saxon text of the canons would have been that used by Wulfsige in addressing his country clergy, as Ælfric states in his Latin letter to Wulfsige accompanying the canons.

Easter table (gerum: a ruled page), a pastoral book, a penitential and a reading book (with the lessons for mattins, etc.). The priest shall have mass vestments (mæsse reaf), and these and his altar cloth must not be torn or dirty. The chalice shall be of pure material and incorruptible (i.e. not of wood), and the paten (disc), and the corporal clean. The mass priest shall, on Sundays, tell the people the sense of the gospel in English, and as often as he can the Pater Noster and the creed also: 'blind is the teacher if he have no book learning'.

The holy fathers appointed also that men pay their tithes to the church. . . . Let the priest go thither (to the harvest field where the tenth sheaf is being collected as tithe), and divide them into three: one for repair of the church, one for the poor, one for God's servants (monks or canons of the old minster, to whom the parochia originally belonged).

Then follows prohibitions of priestly omissions or offences, such as letting a child die unbaptised, taking money for baptism or any other priestly service, getting drunk, wearing weapons, frequenting taverns, buying and selling. The priest must shrive sinners, housel the sick (but not the half-living, for Christ said the housel should be eaten): he must have the chrism for children (to be baptised) and holy oil for the sick.

There were four synods 'for the true faith against heretics': Nicaea, Constantinople, Ephesus and Chalcedon, and these four synods are to be observed in Christ's church, so as the four Christ's books (i.e. the gospels). Then follows a long discourse on the celebration of Easter: 'Now ye have heard authoritatively what ye ought to do and what ye ought to forgo: we cannot make you do it, but wish to be clean at the judgment of God.'

This set of canons for priests is an almost complete statement of their obligations and duties; it is to be supposed that it was solemnly promulged by Wulfsige in synod, and would have no need to be repeated in his episcopate. At later synods, the bishop would address the clergy, hear complaints of wrongs done to priests, or complaints against them. The whole business of determining the exact boundaries of parishes was carried out as a result of the enforcement of the payment of tithe, to one minster or another, or to the local church with graveyard: and disputes about boundaries are likely to have provided business for the diocesan synod. In the normal routine, that is, the issue of a new code of canons for priests was exceptional, as was the issue of a new code of laws in the witan.

The so-called 'Canons enacted under king Edgar' deal only with injunctions for priests (not bishops), and would seem to have been issued in a diocesan synod. Yet the heading in the Old English version of the Cambridge manuscript containing them runs: 'These following (canons) belong now to the law of Edgar, concerning men in orders, how they should live', which seems to imply issue in a witan. It is unlikely however that so long a code applying to priests only would have been published in a witan; also it had a structure, the first clause beginning 'we teach or enjoin' (we lærath), and each succeeding clause beginning 'and we lærath'; the technical, canonical term suggests that the code was compiled for a diocesan synod. The code begins:[1]

> We enjoin ... that at every synod they (the priests) have each year books and vestments for divine service and ink and vellum for their ordinances: and food for three days.
>
> We enjoin that every priest at the synod have his clerk and an orderly man for servant.
>
> We enjoin that every priest in the synod declare if aught be prejudicial to him and if any man have highly injured him: and let them all take it up as if it had been done to them all, and so aid that 'bot' be made, as the bishop shall direct.
>
> And we enjoin that every priest declare in the synod if, in his shrift-shire, he knows any man openly contumacious to God, or miserably sunk in deadly sin, whom he cannot incline to 'bot', or dare not, for worldly opinion.

A long collection of 67 canons follows, wherein the bishop specifies the pastoral duties of his priests. If the manuscript ascription to the reign of Edgar be accepted, Dunstan may indeed have compiled and issued it; Edgar appointed him to the see of Worcester in 959, and that of London in the same year: he became archbishop in 960. The manuscript containing the canons has been attributed indeed to Worcester, or a dependent house; and the clause, 'And we enjoin that every priest, in addition to his learning, diligently learn a handicraft', is the source of the statement in many lives of Dunstan that

---

[1] Thorpe's *Anc. Laws*, i. 395. In C.C.C. Camb. MS. 201, this collection precedes the *Northumbrian Priests' Law*: see Liebermann, *Gesetze*, i. 194.

he required village priests to learn a handicraft, so that they might teach their people. The compiler of the code, in any case, clearly borrowed many injunctions from the *Capitula* of Theodulf of Orleans,[1] as those concerning the bringing of vestment and books to the synod, the care of the altar bread, wine and vessels, the teaching of young clerks, etc.

Among the injunctions of the *Canons*, it is laid down that no priest shall receive another's scholar, implying that some rural priests or canons of a minster educated young clerks individually: this was actually enjoined in the *Capitula* of Theodulf on all rural priests. (Priests in vills and villages should have schools and teach their letters to small children of the parish whose parents commend them to him: nor should he ask any price.) Further: that no learned priest put to shame the half-learned; and no high-born priest despise the lower born; that every child in the priest's shrift-shire be baptised within 37 days, and that no one be too long unbishopped (unconfirmed); that every priest totally extinguish heathenism, well-worshipping and necromancies and man-worshipping, and the delusions that are carried out with spells and heathen sanctuaries, and with elders and some other trees and with stones, that men use for doing many things that they should not; that every Christian man teach his children Pater Noster and the creed; Sundays to be properly kept; no ordeals on feast days or fast days; no priest to celebrate mass save on a hallowed altar, and to have good and rightly written (altar) books, and to have the housel ever ready for those that need it, never to use a wooden chalice but a molten one; no mass priest or minster priest to come near the altar without his proper vestment; priests must diligently teach youth, and educate them in crafts, and every Sunday preach to the people; and remind the people about God's dues; and guard against drunkenness in themselves or other men; and no priest to be an 'ale scop', nor in anywise act the gleeman, but act as becoming his order; no priest to love over much the presence of women, but to love his lawful spouse, his church; and many other points which have much in common with the canons of Ælfric, and the continental canon books as known in England. The canons afford a good picture of the life and duties of the parish priest at the date: the ideal he should hold to, and the temptations likely to befall him. They afford a good picture too of the villager's

[1] See PL. 105. 191–208.

life, with the church and her festivals marking out his year, the church the most dignified building in his village, and the church's directions for his good conduct almost as binding as the king's laws.

The third set of quasi-diocesan canons occur in the same Cambridge manuscript,[1] along with the *Canons enacted under king Edgar* and a great collection of the homilies of Wulfstan. The injunctions are made to priests only: there is no preamble: but the Old English text is headed: *The Law of the Northumbrian Priests*. The word 'law', and the fact that the author of the code announces himself in the first clause as 'God's messenger' (Godes forboda) suggest that this code, though concerning priests, not bishops, was published by king or prince in some northern witan or council. The wording is curious: as is the omission of the normal 'we lærath' before each clause: indeed, the first clause has the royal 'bid' and 'forbid'. It is of course possible that the scribe omitted the 'we lærath' before each clause in weariness, or that he used a transcript of the enactments where it had already been omitted. The suggestion remains however that this episcopal, or more probably archiepiscopal, code had some sort of royal sanction or even publishing. The title, the use of the Danish coins, the ora and the mark, and some other terms give the scope of the code as 'Northumbrian', i.e. north of the Humber: it is accepted by Liebermann as issued from York, the place named in one clause defining travel limits.

The 67 canons (laws) are constantly concerned with the amount of the bot or fine for offences by a priest or against a priest. In these *Northumbrian Priests' Laws*, it is laid down that if any priest is injured, all his fellow priests, with the bishop's help, shall diligently see that he is compensated, that they be 'all of one heart and one mind'. No priest shall buy the church of another. A priest neglecting the edict of his bishop shall pay 20 oras, and one making a payment to a lay person to get himself ordained, 20 oras. If a priest neglect an archdeacon's edict, 12 oras. If a priest is guilty of a crime, and celebrates mass without the archdeacon's edict, 12 oras; if he refuses baptism or to hear a confession, let him compensate with 12 oras. If a priest do not seek the chrism at the proper time, 12 oras. Each child shall be baptised within nine days: if not, six oras. If a child die unbaptised

---

[1] C.C.C. Camb. MS. 201; see Thorpe, *Anc. Laws*, i. 416; Liebermann, *Gesetze*, i. 380, where C.C.C. Camb. MS. 201 is dated as c. 1060; Darlington, 412.

within nine days through negligence, the parents shall make amends
to God without worldly fine; if it were over nine days, the parents
shall make amends to God and pay 12 oras to their parish priest.
A list of fines payable in oras is also included for such offences as a
priest's wrongly announcing to his people a feast or fast, celebrating
in an unconsecrated building, using a wooden cup for the eucharist,
celebrating without wine, neglecting the holy eucharist. Fines are
also specified for those who fight in church, hold a market in church,
eject a priest unjustly from his church; if any man wound a priest, he
shall compensate by having the wound cared for, and pay compensation to the altar, 12 oras for a priest, six for a deacon. If one priest
fight another, he shall compensate both him and the bishop; if a
priest neglect to shear his beard and hair, he shall pay a fine; if a
priest 'deserts his concubine and takes another, he shall be accursed'
(this tacitly recognises the status of the priest's housekeeper-wife), if
he do not ring the bell and sing the hours at the proper time, he shall
pay a fine; so also if he covers up his tonsure (e.g. in the tavern), gets
drunk habitually, conceals any unjust compact between men in his
parish, omits the yearly rites through forgetfulness, neglects to go
to the synod, be openly hostile to the bishop's decree, etc.

We all ought to venerate and love God, and diligently preserve
one Christianity and altogether reject paganism. If anyone is known
to do anything pagan, either by sortilege or (magical) writings, or
if he worship an idol, if he be a king's thegn let him pay 10 half
marks, half to Christ, half to the king; and any other landed possessor,
six half marks, or peasant, 12 oras. If a king's thegn deny this, then
let 12 oath helpers be nominated for him, and let him take 12 of his
kin and 12 'pilgrims', as oath helpers: if he fail, let him pay the fine.
If he be a landed possessor or a peasant, he must clear himself by oath
helpers.

A clearer picture of pagan practices is afforded by canon liv
(which is paralleled in a Carolingian code): 'If there be a gathering
for pagan superstition (conventus superstitiosus) on any man's land,
around a stone, or around a tree, or a spring, or any other foolish-
nesses (nugae) of this kind: then let the leader pay the penalty for
breaking the law, half to Christ, half to the landowner. And if the
landlord be not willing to help this discipline, then Christ and the
king shall have the penalty due.

Further, we prohibit buying and selling on Sunday, and all

assembling of the people and all work, and all travel, as well with carts as with horses and with loads. Penalty: a free man, 12 oras; a slave shall be beaten: except for pilgrims, who must needs leave the district. And it is lawful to set forth for war on the vigils of feasts, if need arise, for a district of six miles around York.

We wish also that each man pay his Rome penny (Peter's pence) around the feast of St. Peter's chair (Feb. 22). We will also that in each wapentake there shall be nominated two faithful thegns and one priest to collect it and pass it on, on oath; and if any king's thegn or landed possessor dare to detain it, he shall pay 10 half marks. Penalty for the reeve or steward (villaticus) who detains or conceals Peter's pence (stated); for a king's thegn who detains tithe, etc.

No one to marry within the fourth degree, or to marry their baptismal sponsor ... or to put away his lawful wife and take another wife.

The injunctions and enactments of these codes, and of the ecclesiastical clauses of the secular laws, are explained and commented on in the *Institutes of polity*, a long tract written by some scholar bishop some time later than the days of Edgar: the chapter 'On reeves' states that it is right that reeves should seek to provide for and profit their lords, 'but now it has been altogether too much the case, since Edgar died, as God willed, that there are more robbers than righteous: it is grievous that those who should be the guardians of Christian people should be robbers'. The concluding paragraph of chapter 21, dealing with priests, ends: 'Beloved men, do as I, for the love of God and Saint Mary, beseech you.'

The first chapters express Dunstan's concept of the Christian monarchy: 'It befits a Christian king in a Christian nation, to be, as is right, the people's comfort and a righteous shepherd over a Christian flock. And it is his duty, with all his power, to uprear Christendom, with just laws as he diligently may; he shall chastise evil-doing men with secular punishment, and all God's foes sternly withstand.' He shall be mild to the good and stern to the evil. He shall meditate wisdom with his witan; it behoves kings and bishops, earls and 'heretogan' (dukes), reeves and those who deal dooms, doctors and lawyers, to be of one mind in the witan.

Bishops are beadles (heralds) and teachers of God's law: he contemns God who contemns God's preachers. Bishops shall follow their book and their prayers, and intercede for all Christian people. To a bishop belongs all direction both in divine and worldly things. He shall not consent to any injustice, and priests in their shrift-shires shall diligently support every right, and never permit that any Christian man injure another, not the higher the lower, nor the shire man those under him, nor the lord his men nor even his thralls (servi): we are all God's own thralls, and so will He judge us as we here judge those over whom we have judgment on earth. Every bishop shall have the book of canons at the synod, and be ye unanimous, and let each defend other behind his back. Bishops shall have wise men (witan) to travel with them, and let there always be good instruction in their families.

Priests are exhorted at length how to lead and defend the people of their shrift-shire, preaching and giving instruction. Laymen are exhorted to chastity before marriage and to have one wife only, and preferably not to marry again after her death. Then follows a long discourse on Constantine the great emperor and his synod of Nicaea, and the other three great synods, and others about our one spiritual mother: 'she is named ecclesia: that is, God's church', and we should love and honour her. It is right that every (local) church be in God's grith: every church grith is Christ's own grith. 'Let every man constantly take care that he do not too greatly misuse the bride of Christ.'[1]

Many injunctions are found in these royal codes and the tenth century reformers' writings about the celibacy of the clergy, as required by the canons from early days. It is equally clear that royal and episcopal injunctions never succeeded in securing the celibacy of priests and deacons, at least apart from those living in communities of monks and strict canons. Though the reformers tended to accuse priests who were not celibate of living disreputable lives with one woman after another, there is evidence that married clergy in the countryside were held in respect and spoken of as married. The New Minster at Winchester, for instance, inscribed certain married priests, with their wives, their sons and daughters, as among their bene-factors as a matter of course, which would not have been possible if the marriage of the clergy was held at the time a matter of scandal. The *Liber Vitae* of the New Minster included a list of those who had had a peculiar devotion to their minster, beginning with an abbot of

---

[1] See Thorpe, B., *Anc. Laws*, i. 422-440.

the community of Ghent, and continuing with many other abbots, priests, and monks of other houses, in great numbers; among the 'sacerdotes' occur 'Godwinus the priest and his wife Erenburch and his sons Stigand and Tove', and 'Æfhelmus the priest and Osmund and their wives and sons and daughters'.

That rural priests were married with no discredit is indicated by the will made by a lady just going off on pilgrimage, sometime in the first half of the eleventh century. Siflæd's will ends with the direction: 'And my church is to be free, and Wulfmær my priest is to sing at it, he and his issue, so long as they are in holy orders.'[1] Similarly, the abbot of Burton-on-Trent, a strict monastery founded at the beginning of the eleventh century by a wealthy thegn of the northern Danelaw, Wulfric Spott, depended for the care of the abbey's parish upon a succession of married chaplains. The earliest charters in the Burton cartulary which refer to the provision of a priest to serve the parish of Burton are post-Conquest, of c. 1114 and c. 1159;[2] but though the parish chaplain in c. 1114 swore the feudal oath of homage to the abbot, receiving certain emoluments for his service, the implication is that he was succeeding to his father's chaplaincy, in succession to a line of chaplains who would have sworn the old hold oath of loyalty. The first chaplain whose name occurs in the charters, and earlier than c. 1114, is a certain Recelbert (?Æthelberht), who had four acres of inland, hospitality from the abbot, the allowance of one monk in hay for his horse from the abbot's courtyard, and a share in the tithes of Burton. Before 1126 there was a priest Ælwin at Burton who had a croft (? of fruit trees); and in the charter of c. 1114, abbot Geoffrey of Burton grants to Ælwin the priest, son of Ælwin, four bovates of land, the chaplaincy of the church 'to serve the parish as long as he lives'; he shall have the 'procuration of one monk' (food and clothing allowance), and a prebend of food for his horse from the abbey courtyard and a house outside the monastery gate 'as his father had, that he may fill his office with prudence'. That this Ælwin was a married priest is shown by a charter of c. 1188, when abbot Nicholas confirmed possession of the four bovates to 'Vincent, son of Ælwin the priest and his heirs ... as his father and grandfather held them'. The various

[1] ASWills, no. 37.
[2] See Jeayes, I. H., *Charters and Muniments belonging to the marquis of Anglesey*, in Staffordshire Rec. Soc. vol. for 1936, pp. liv and nos. 7 and 24.

grants concerning the chaplaincy show that Ælwin and his son Vincent and the pre-Conquest chaplains held their office like any other tenant who had sworn the hold oath; they served a large parish (by modern standards), using the minster church, or its nave, as their parish church; they had by c. 1159 four bovates of land in the common fields, a house in Stapenhill (about a mile from the abbey), with a croft of pear trees and one acre of land near the house, the procuration of one monk and the prebend for one horse and a 'hospice' outside the monastery gate. There is no evidence that the succession of the sons of married priests serving the parish of Burton was exceptional or regarded as disastrous; there must have been many similar cases.

CHAPTER VIII

THE INFLUENCE OF THE ROMAN CIVIL SERVICE ON ECCLESIASTICAL ADMINISTRATION

THE secular laws in pre-Conquest England were announced to the witan in Old English, and written down in that language in the codes. Linguistically and by their ancestry they may fairly be counted as Germanic, just as the moots that did justice, witan and shire moot and hundred moot, were Germanic institutions. The invading Anglo-Saxons and Jutes had however lived on the borders of the Roman empire, and perhaps passed years in their journey through north Germany and the Low Countries; they had seen villas owned by individuals or the imperial fisc and cultivated by 'coloni': they had some knowledge of late Roman institutions and private property in land. It has been credibly suggested that the invaders of Kent must have found villas and the territories of the fisc, their cultivators not all fled to Brittany though the villa owners had: and that such landed estates passed to kings, kinglets and the nobility of birth. Kings had lived in palaces and nobles in halls of their own, even in the heroic poetry of the Germanic past. There must, from the times of the Anglo-Saxon settlement have been some influence of late Roman institutions and Roman vulgar law[1] upon the English invaders; but before Augustine came there was no writing down of Anglo-Saxon law, which might, conceivably, have shown Roman influence. Even though the 'book' or written conveyance of individual property, lands or rights came in the seventh century, undoubtedly following a late Roman legal procedure, it would be still true to say that the enunciation of Anglo-Saxon laws in the witan did not follow Roman forms. Secular law remained, broadly speaking, Germanic.

Among ecclesiastics, however, members of a church as wide as the known world of the day and chiefly functioning in what had

[1] See E. Levy's *West Roman Vulgar Law: the law of property*, 1951: though the author deals only with the Continent, the book is of interest to the student of early English institutions.

once been the Roman empire, there was always some knowledge of Roman law: knowledge of the Theodosian Code of 438. This code had long sections dealing with the imperial civil service, with the different grades of officials, their titles, salaries, the honour due to them and the nature of their work. There was much about the imperial notaries or legal scribes, of whom the cancellarius (chancellor) was one variety. Not only the emperors continued to have a bureau of notaries, but the great secular officials under them, the new barbarian kings in Europe, and the pope and the bishops. Knowledge of the Theodosian code was disseminated in the west by the notaries, and church law, being international, followed Roman law more closely than the new Germanic codes did. While the codes of the Ostrogoths, Visigoths and Lombards show the influence of Roman vulgar law (the Theodosian Code was itself no longer classical Roman law, but influenced by the vulgar law of the Roman provinces), yet these new Germanic codes had an ancestry of their own, besides the vulgar law: whereas the church, in her canonical procedure, had not. She tried to adapt Roman law to be a vehicle of the Christian ethic. In the business of ecclesiastical administration in particular, she adopted the methods and, in some cases the names, of Roman imperial officials. The notaries, above all, were useful to her.

As to the amount of legal knowledge possessed by the Anglo-Saxons: Augustine brought a band of monks and, as far as we know, no notary. But he had himself been provost of a Roman monastery, familiar with the duty of maintaining property and feeding the household from revenue or alms. With archbishop Theodore came the notary Titillus, and scarcely without some books of Roman law. The English church, from the days of Theodore and Wilfrid had a notarial knowledge of Roman law.

In the long history of the influence of Roman law on church law, two points are of special importance for England: pope Gregory I's influence on the taking over of the traditions and work of the Roman civil service by the clerical order, and the tenth century borrowing of the title of 'dean', with its legal implications, from the imperial civil service.

As to the administrative technique of the pre-Conquest church: much of it was notarial technique, acquired by the deliberate policy

of England's patron, pope Gregory I. Many of the officers and
official terms used in the pre-Conquest church were in fact borrowed
from the Greco-Roman civil service: the technique used by the
bishop's deacons for the transaction of business: terms like 'rector'
as the ruler of the land of a local church: the 'patroni' and 'posses-
sores' of the private churches, and the 'defensores' of the greater
churches and minsters. Pope Gregory I had passed up the ladder of
the civil service himself and was completely familiar with its work
and its methods: it was during his pontificate that the work of
notaries and clerks was increasingly assimilated, notably in the case
of the papal deacons.

The taking over by the church of the transmission of education
and the practice of Roman law in the west was of course due to the
disappearance of the rhetors' schools in the fifth century, and the gap
left in lay education. In the Byzantine east the civil service was still
manned by laymen: but in the west bishops had to educate their
clergy from boyhood in their own household schools. There were
no other schools. A few merchants learned to write and keep
accounts as part of their trade, and in agriculture the peasant bailiffs
sometimes learned enough writing to keep their tallies and renders
(though often enough they simply retained them in their heads, or
by means of notches on gate posts). But in Sicily, where the papacy
had landed estates, Gregory I's bailiffs or 'conductores' learned
enough writing to understand his many detailed letters of instruction, and it seemed to Gregory that they should therefore be entitled
to the privileges of the clerical order. He commanded that they
should be given the tonsure, and this was a landmark: for it was the
first time the tonsure had been given to men not intending to go on
at least to minor orders.

He pursued the same policy with the more important rulers of
estates in the patrimony: they had been trained as civil servants, and
had civil service titles: they were now ordained to some grade in the
clerical militia. In the great collection of Gregory's letters that has
survived to us, there are many references to notaries and some letters
addressed to them. His letters about the administration of the
different patrimonies of the Roman church show that the manage-
ment of local estates, such as had in the past been committed by the
emperors (and were still committed by the Germanic kings) to
'domestics' and 'counts', were now committed by Gregory to

'rectores' or 'defensores' (of a smaller estate, a 'possessiuncula'), or to custodians designated simply as 'notary'. The rectors of patrimonies were all deacons and sub-deacons (except Candidus, the rector of the patrimony in Gaul, who was a priest). The defensores appear to have been sub-deacons. This incorporated them into the papal familia: the scrinium itself remained a body of lay notaries.

In Anglo-Saxon England, the deacons became, as in Rome, the most important executive officers of an episcopal familia. While most pastoral work outside the bishop's see town was carried on by the minsters, little distant supervision was needed and the deacons severally could write grants and letters as the bishop needed. It was when the increase of rural parishes made the personal horseback journeys of the bishop insufficient, that the need of an archdeacon or archdeacons (with the use of other than the bishop's horses) was desirable.

As to the tenth century borrowing of the old civil service title of dean: this attests the reformers' knowledge of the section defining the duties of deans in the Theodosian Code. The clergy had learned from it the titles and functions of the various Byzantine civil servants; they learned about the different varieties of notaries: the 'cancellarii', who were at first ushers in the law courts: the head of the department of notaries, the primicerius (who was 'a two hundred a year man' and 'merited on retirement to wear the ceremonial purple'), and the secundicerius; the numerarii, who dealt with the revenue and ranked as knights; they learned about the dean (decanus, dekanos).

The Theodosian Code[1] is almost certainly the link between what the dean was in the fourth, fifth and sixth centuries, and what he was deemed to be in the Carolingian period, and in ninth and tenth century England. In the first period there were several varieties of dean, all part of central or city or provincial administration, beside the deans in the army, and they were all laymen; in the second, in the ninth and tenth centuries, the deans were all clergy: either the deans of cathedrals or monasteries, or the rural deans who on the Continent in the ninth century superseded the archpriests in their territorial archpriesteries. (In England, the subdivision of sees into archdeaconries and rural deaneries did not come till the twelfth century.)

[1] For the status and work of deans in this code, see *infra*, p. 157.

It has been a matter of historical speculation why the title 'dean' was first used in the west: if 'decanus' was derived from 'decem', what constituted the 10 over which these deans presided? Did a cathedral dean preside over 10 canons? Or a monastic dean over 10 monks? Historically, he did not. Did a rural dean, on the Continent, preside over 10 parishes? Historically, no.[1] To the ninth and tenth century clergy the 'decanus' had no connotation with 10: they took him over with the connotations of the title in Roman law and the great code.

This connotation turns upon the derivation of decanus, and its usage, at the times the two codes were compiled. The old view was that 'decanus' was then associated with 'decem': but actually, it was back in the Republican period that a decurio in the Roman army had had under him a group of 10 soldiers, and had himself served under a centurion. When, six centuries and more later, the Theodosian Code was compiled, the Roman civil servant, the dean, was a kind of messenger, a receiver of papers from a government department, who bore them to the emperor. M. Robert Guilland in 1947 claimed that 'dekanos' had two roots: the old 'deka' and the deponent verb 'dechomai' (I receive);[2] a dean in the Byzantine civil service, he claimed, was an official messenger, summoned at will to the imperial presence, or bearing imperial commands to the emperor's subjects; of this he gave several historical instances. While M. Guilland's merit as a historian of the Byzantine civil service commands respect, his derivation of dekanos from dechomai appears at first sight doubtful: but philologists explain that by a mysterious process called 'popular etymology' a word has often become associated with two root words, or with a root with which it had philologically no connexion. In popular speech, a word derived from one root came to be associated with another: the barriers of meaning broke down and the two sets of association fused. By the time of St. Ambrose, who received an imperial message to give up the basilica Portiana to the Arians at the hands of two deans,[3] the dean was a messenger; in the Code of 438 he bore papers from the

---

[1] See Thompson, A. Hamilton, 'Archdeacons and rural deans', in the Raleigh Lecture, given as a Brit. Acad. lecture for 1945; he proved the taking over of the local archpriesteries by the rural deans, but does not deal with the question, why the title dean was used.

[2] See his 'Le Décanos et le référendaire' in the *Rev. des Études Byzantines*, v (1947), 91.

[3] See *Sancti Ambrosii ep.* i. 20, in PL. xvi, col. 995.

notariat to the emperor and vice versa. He had an importance
because the person with access to the sovereign was more important
than those who wrote the papers in the department: but he was not
one of the great officials.[1]

In the monasticism of the Greek east, Jerome speaks of monks
(*Ep.* 20) as divided into 'decaniae': and Augustine of monks
working under 'decani'. In the well known 21st chapter of St.
Benedict's rule, similarly, St. Benedict stated that it was preferable
that monks, under their abbot, should be entrusted to several deans
rather than one provost; M. Guilland argued that he was speaking
of deans in the contemporary sense, as in Roman law, as of lesser
officials intermediary between a superior and a group, and with no
reference to 10: as in the Theodosian Code and that of Justinian.
There is no decisive evidence about St. Benedict's use of the word.

The Byzantine church also had secular deans, minor officials, who
might receive the offerings of the faithful and divide them out to the
priests and clerics of the church. They might be, as it were, the head
vergers of the church, the chief of its secular attendants: they are
several times described as 'rod-bearers'; the patriarch had such an
usher. There are many instances to show that in the time of St.
Benedict, and much earlier, the dissociation of deans from any
function connected with 10 was quite normal, and that they were
commonly associated with the function of messenger or official go-
between.

This was their function in the Theodosian Code and that of
Justinian. The deans were a kind of official messenger corps, a *schola*
or college working under the supervision of the 'Magister Offici-
orum': they acted as ushers, rod-bearers, within the palace and were
sometimes sent on minor missions. They ranked as the first grade in
the civil service: four of them might rank as primiceries for the space
of two years, after which they were to return to the general body of
deans, letting four others succeed them.[2] They attained the position
of primicery by seniority; a precedent in *lex Romana* for a dean as
temporary president which possibly affected the election of Caro-

---

[1] There were still military deans in the Visigothic army, modelled on the Roman
army: deans who deserted their 'decaneias' should pay 10 solidi to the court: MGH.
Legum 1; *Lex Visigothorum*, 9. 2. 4. Vegetius, in his *De Arte Militari* (ii. 8, p. 13)
mentions these army deans ; in the Byzantine army they were called 'dekarchs'.

[2] *Theodosiani libri xvi*, ed. T. Mommsen and P. M. Mayer, Berlin, 1905: Bk. *vi.*
xxxiii. 1, p. 303.

lingian rural deans by seniority or the vote of their fellow parish priests: the rural dean was not sufficiently important for the bishop to insist on appointing him.

As far as pre-Conquest sources can determine, 'decanus' was as often used as the style of an abbot's second in command as of a bishop's in the last century before 1066: the ASC. and the attestations of charters, that is, refer to such a person sometimes as a dean, sometimes as provost, but not as a prior. St. Benedict conceded, however, that the abbot might appoint a 'praepositus' as his helper if the monks desired it and he himself judged it wise. There is no obstacle to the appointment of a provost in the Benedictine rule. What is found however in this period in England is a single official, who at need made his attestation as dean; or, at times, as provost. In Roman law, the title 'dean' as implying an intermediary between a superior and his subjects, would be as applicable to a dean under an abbot as a dean under a bishop: and it would seem that monastic deans at the time were the deans of the Roman law books.

The term provost, praepositus, occurs sometimes in attestations to charters, as it does in the rule of Chrodegang, as a possible title for the head of a community of canons. Cuthbert had held the office of 'praepositus' of the guests' hospitium at Ripon[1] and praepositus of the community at Lindisfarne. Provost, in short, was the normal term for the abbot's second in command up till the days of the monastic reform under Æthelwold. In tenth century England there were, besides the provosts, monastic deans intermediary between the abbot and his monks, a single intermediary. The precedent of Roman law might allow of the dean's attaining the position by seniority or monastic election, but Benedictine practice and the fact that he was the abbot's right hand suggest rather that the abbot nominated him: there is no decisive evidence. On the whole, temporary presidency, whether by seniority or election, was a device of Roman law, and when society became feudalised, it was unlikely to survive. Even in the case of Carolingian rural deans, the bishop came eventually to appoint them.

The passage about deans and their primiceries in the Theodosian Code has two other points of historical interest. It accords with the modern usage of the word 'doyen', as presiding over the diplomatic corps by seniority; and it throws light on the medieval and modern

[1] Plummer, i. xxviii, nn. 4, 5.

use of 'dean' as applied to a bishop as official messenger, as it were, between the archbishop and the bishops of his province. The bishop of London was, and still is, dean of the province of Canterbury. He takes papers, in the manner of the dean of Roman law, from the archbishop to the provincial bishops; he issues the archbishop's summons to the provincial synod. He has access to the archbishop and executes his commands to the province.

CHAPTER IX

ARCHDEACONS AND DEANS

It is hardly surprising that the Christian church should have taken over much of her territorial arrangements from those of the Roman empire at its collapse in the west in the fifth century: the church had to deal with population groups as they existed at the time. It is however rather surprising that, three or four centuries later, she should still have looked for guidance in manners of administration to the old Roman civil service with its notaries and other officers, as in fact she did. Perhaps it is the less surprising as the see of Peter and the old capital of Constantine were still part of the Byzantine, Mediterranean world, inheriting and living by the old Greco-Roman tradition. Civilitas and Romanitas went together: there were many notaries who knew Roman law and the old formulae: lay people, but very civilised. The see of Peter, the bishops and all the barbarian rulers of the west except the English, made much use of notaries; in England, as well as in other west European kingdoms, the clergy learned the notarial technique together with some of the rules of Roman law; eventually, the deacons in episcopal households took over the work of the notaries. The bishop's deacons, trained in notarial practice in their long passage through the orders of subdeacon and deacon, took over much of the bishop's administrative work, though only in a few sees in our period in England was the term 'archdeacon' used, and not as yet with a territorial significance. As to 'deans', the title was derived from the Roman law books, though its use was popularised by the rule of St. Benedict. There were, that is, before the Norman Conquest in England, plenty of deans of minsters, cathedral and other; there were as yet no rural deans.

To consider first then the work of the deacons and archdeacons: for the deacon was from the first an order in the Christian ministry, while the dean (decanus or dekanos) was a Roman civil servant, whose work and status were carefully set down in the two great codes of Roman law. The deacon's work was important in this late

Old English period for the observance of canonical order in the parishes: when every journey was a journey on horseback, the bishop by now needed help in the supervision of his rural parishes, which were increasing in number. It was the deacon's or archdeacon's task to ensure that the rural clergy observed the canons passed in synod or witan, and to do the bishop's writing work.

Deacons in fifth and sixth century Europe had acquired a semi-notarial technique. From the time of Constantine, bishops had owned property and been called upon to give quasi-legal decisions when their clergy were accused of crime or involved in law suits: they had needed the services of lawyers and every bishop employed one or two notaries. Gradually, the deacons took over notarial work.

The bishops had used their deacons for their pastoral duty of distributing alms, and the deacons had become involved in administrative business with the notaries who wrote the bishop's letters, issued his summons to the synod and recorded its *acta*. Pope Gregory the Great associated the work of the deacons with that of the notaries yet more closely (see *supra*, p. 139) and finally insisted that certain notaries should be ordained to the grade of deacon. Though at Rome the papal bureau of notaries, the scrinium, continued throughout the middle ages as the official writing office and archive department of the papacy, the chief deacon (at Rome called 'the seventh deacon') became his chief executive, legal, officer. The chief deacon, or archdeacon, became similarly all over western Europe, the bishop's chief legal officer (till, in the thirteenth century, his duty of presiding over the bishop's court was taken over by the 'official'). The favourite medieval joke about the worldliness of archdeacons had this much historical justification: the archdeacon had a double ancestry. Biblical study derived his office from that of St. Stephen in the Acts: but his other ancestor, the Roman notary, was always looking over his shoulder.

In England, in the period between the tenth century reform and 1066, a bishop might apparently use any of the deacons of his familia for quasi-legal, administrative work. In the primatial sees of Canterbury and York, the need for the delegation of episcopal work led, at least under some archbishops, to the use of the term 'archdeacon' for the senior among the deacons: perhaps to only one of them (at York?). The 'archdeacon' on the Continent in the fifth and sixth centuries had been simply the chief among the deacons, as the arch-priest had been the chief of the presbyters and the primicerius that of the lectors or notaries.[1] The archdeacon, though he was the chief officer of the bishop and more important than any of the presbyters, remained normally in deacon's orders: it was not held fitting that a priest should immerse himself unduly in worldly business.[2] The closeness of the chief, or arch, deacon's relationship to the bishop, whose right hand man he was, determined his importance. When, much later, a see came to be divided into territorial archdeaconries, the 'archidiaconus maior' was always the archdeacon of the cathedral church, in close relations with the bishop. In Italy, where sees were small, the 'archidiaconus maior' was normally the only archdeacon; in western Europe, where sees were much larger, the need to devolve episcopal work and supervision was the chief cause of the multiplica-tion of archdeaconries. In England, there was need to devolve episcopal supervision, at least at Canterbury and York: but no terri-torial subdivision of any see was made for a century after the Norman Conquest.

The evidence for the existence of archdeacons at Canterbury is fuller than in the case of York, and earlier: it belongs to the ninth century when archbishop Hincmar of Reims was already dividing his great see into territorial archdeaconries and further into rural deaneries. The territorial archdeacon was one of the bishop's deacons, planted out in the most important church of his area: his church was his benefice. The rural 'dean' might be elected from among them-selves by the priests of his smaller area, though later the bishop appointed him: he was specifically the bearer of papers, the messenger, between the local priests and the bishop: he had nothing to do with monasteries or St. Benedict's rule: his title was a notarial title. There were as yet no rural deans in England: but in the tenth century reform the Continental, notarial use of dean was adopted for the intermediary between minster and bishop, or minster and abbot.

There are four authentic charters of archbishop Ceolnoth (833–870) signed by three or four archdeacons in each case, and there is good reason to believe that they were not strangers, but members of

[1] See 'The archdeacons of Canterbury under archbishop Ceolnoth, (833–870)', by Deanesly, M., in the EHR. clxv (1927), 1-11.
[2] Though archbishop Hincmar of Reims in 877 addressed two of his 'archdeacon priests' in an important commission, it did not become general for archdeacons to be in priests' orders till the twelfth century: see PL. 125, col. 799.

the archbishop's familia. The Kentish charters at the time were attested by lists of clergy more complete than at any other period: they include bishops, presbyters, deacons and clerks in minor orders: it is possible by comparison of these charters to tell which clergy belonged to the archbishop's familia at Christ Church, and which to the familiae of the minsters at Folkestone, Lyminge, Dover, Reculver, etc.: though these familiae were also regarded as, in a certain sense, belonging to the archbishop. By comparing the lists of clergy who attested the charters, it is possible in some cases to trace a particular clerk as passing up from one clerical order to another: and when he finally attested charters as 'archidiaconus', it is safe to assume that he was an archdeacon of Christ Church, where he had passed through the ecclesiastical orders. Clerks can similarly be traced passing up the different grades in the charters of a few other churches, e.g. that of Worcester.

There is some evidence that in England the special nature of the work of the bishop's deacons was recognised, whether or not the chief deacons of his familia received the title 'archdeacon': as some did in the ninth century in the households of the archbishops of Canterbury. Here, particularly in archbishop Ceolnoth's time, grants and leases were signed often by the whole familia (hired, hird), or a substantial part of it. In four cases between 863 and 870 three, or four, archdeacons signed: and, in one grant signed by archbishop Ceolnoth,[1] Cialbarht[2] signed as 'presbyter diaconus'; he signed after a priest Sigefreth, and the archdeacons Sigefreth and Ealhstan. The priest Sigefreth had been an archdeacon in an earlier charter, and the second Sigefreth and Ealhstan had signed as archdeacons earlier: Cialbarht, signing between them and the two sub-deacons, would seem to have been a priest doing deacon's work.[3] The senior Sigefreth had been promoted priest and may have been no longer doing the work of a deacon.

⎨ The appointment of archdeacons at Canterbury, and a single archdeacon at York, the two primatial sees from which the bishop must

---

[1] Cotton MS. Augustus II. 19: see BCS., no. 404.

[2] The apparently anomalous style 'presbyter diaconus' is explicable when the delegation of the bishop's authority in certain administrative and supervisory matters was recognised. In the later 'Northumbrian Priests' Law', penalties are stated for disobedience to the bishop's edict and the archdeacon's edict: they would not attach to disregard of a letter from a priest of the bishop's familia.

[3] In BCS. no. 516 (the setting up of a see at St. Martin's in 867), Cialbarht signed as sub-deacon.

needs attend the king's court or witan oftener than other bishops, did but emphasise that the work of a bishop's deacon was recognised as that of a special officer. All priests passed through the diaconate, learning there something of notarial practice as well as theology and pastoral care: but some deacons were retained for years for their special aptitude for notarial and supervisory work. Some remained in deacon's orders while doing this work; some like Cialbarht at Canterbury and Goding at Worcester were eventually ordained priests. It is possible that such priests continued to work as bishop's deacons after being so ordained and granted a lease for three lives of land and a house in the episcopal city; there is however little evidence for this in England. On the Continent archdeacons were provided for by the grant of an important church as benefice, to serve which they had need to be in priest's orders: the setting up of territorial archdeaconries provided both for pro-episcopal supervision from a local centre (important where sees were large), and for the mainten-ance of the archdeacon. In England where sees were comparatively small, the bishop's deacon could work from the see city, and the lands leased to him as reward for faithful service entailed no priestly obligations. The bishop's deacon, who served him for years, was, it seems, regarded in England as an important person; when the Winchester version of the ASC. (the Parker Chronicle) records under the year 963 that 'Wulfstan the deacon passed away on Holy Innocents day', it is unlikely that he was just one of the young clergy in training in the Old Minster.

As early as 864 a grant of king Æthelberht of Wessex to the minster at Sherborne was witnessed by 'Torhthelm, diaconus prae-positus', which suggests that Torhthelm was both the bishop's deacon and minster provost of Sherborne.[1] In a grant to St. Augus-tine's abbey of 958, Byrhtsige the deacon signed before the mass priests.[2] But the clearest case of the continued service of the same deacon for years comes from Worcester, with its exceptionally long list of domestic grants, made by bishop Oswald to his thegns, relatives, faithful servants and clerks, attested, as the grant often states, by the members of the 'heored' or familia. Whether the heored was the monastic familia, the monastery he had established in the old minster at Worcester, or the monks plus certain clergy who had not undertaken the monastic obligation, is not clear: but

[1] ASChar. no. 11.   [2] Ib. no. 32.

all the signatories were, in some sense, Oswald's clergy at Worcester. Heored or hird was as often used, at the date, of a monastic community as of a clerical one.

In the long series of Worcester grants (see p. 164), several deacons attested over a number of years: more, apparently than would have been needed by a clerk making a routine passage up to the priesthood. But two clerks especially, Goding and Leofstan, attested as many as 50 grants, both signing as deacons, between the years 965 and 992,[1] the year of Oswald's death. There is an interesting grant,[2] undated except for the reference to Oswald as archbishop, which places it as later than 972, where Oswald grants a lease for three lives to 'his priest Goding', of three hides at 'Bradingcote' and two other local holdings: 'and we book to him the house he has had before the gate, and for two lives after his day'. This is a similar, though a much larger, grant than that made to Oswald's priest, 'Wulfgar by name'. Goding had been attesting grants for years as deacon: Wulfgar several as 'clericus', three times as late as 991.[3] Goding attested no grant as 'presbyter', and if his land grant was made to him before 991, he must have attested (officially) as deacon, though in priest's orders: he so attested a grant to Æthelmær, Oswald's architect (artifex) in 991.[4] It remains uncertain whether Goding and Wulfgar ever attested as deacon and clerk, their office in Oswald's registry, while actually in priest's orders.

At Canterbury in the ninth century there is evidence, first for a single archdeacon (archidiaconus maior) and then for a number of archdeacons. They were general assistants to the bishop and their work was not territorially limited. Archbishop Wulfred (805–832) had himself been archdeacon: he had attested as archdeacon the so-called council of Beccanfield in 803, and charters of archbishop Æthelheard in 805.[5] He succeeded Æthelheard in that year, and it was he who made possible canonical life at Christ Church by providing the familia with a mensa, and building a dormitory and refectory. No charters are attested by an archdeacon between the

---

[1] See BCS. nos. 1166, 1167, 1205, 1299. KCD. nos. 596, 612-620, 623, 625, 627, 630, 634, 637, 644, 645, 646, 649, 651, 653, 660, 661, 666-671, 674-682.
[2] *Ib*. no. 683.   [3] *Ib*. nos. 676-678.
[4] *Ib*. no. 678. It is unlikely that the land grant was made to him before 985, which is the last time 'Wynsige the priest', a famous Worcester dean and monk, attested (see *infra*, p. 165): Goding's grant is not signed by Wynsige.
[5] *Ib*. no. 319.

years 805 and 830, though one of 811 was signed by as many as seven deacons. In 830, however, Cynehard signed as archdeacon, an office he may have been able to support by reason of his own family property: for archbishop Wulfred granted land willed to him by 'Cynehard the deacon' to the Christ Church familia before his own death in 833. There was nothing inconsistent between the strict canonical life, evidently desired by Wulfred for Christ Church, and the office of archdeacon; the Rule of Chrodegang provided for an archdeacon resident in the community, of which he might as arch-deacon be head under the bishop; he might have a separate household, maintained by a 'portion' allotted to him from the community funds: but possibly the Christ Church endowment did not allow of the maintenance of a separate archdeacon's household between the time when Wulfred was able to support the office and Cynehard the deacon had property sufficient to do likewise. The maintenance of a separate household, with at least two or three horses and servants to enable the archdeacon to visit the parishes of the see, was in fact desirable; yet it might well give an appearance of 'worldly pomp' such as the tenth century reformers deprecated. Archbishop Wulfred in fact, by giving Cynehard's archidiaconal 'portion', as family land, to Christ Church, made the work of the archdeacon possible either by one archdeacon or the senior deacons as need arose: there would be the horses and servants to do it.

Archbishop Ceolnoth succeeded Wulfred in 833, after a brief interval when two successors of Wulfred died, one at least of the plague. He accomplished his supervision of rural parishes for some years by himself or the use of his deacons; but a deed of 843, by which king Æthelwulf of the West Saxons and Kent granted land in Kent was signed by archbishop Ceolnoth, Wærheard the pres-byter abbot, and two archdeacons: Wealhere and Nothwulf: the signatures, attached on a slip to the charter, may be a few years later than 843.[1] A single archdeacon, 'Duning', attested a confirmation by king Æthelwulf of the purchase of land in Kent by a Kentish thegn from a Kentish 'dux': neither Ceolnoth nor any clergy certainly of Christ Church attested with him, yet it is difficult to conjecture whose archdeacon he can have been, except Ceolnoth's.[2]

[1] BCS. no. 429; there is a list of signatures to the charter, and in one with the same names on an attached slip the two deacons of the charter have become arch-deacons: they appear in other charters as deacons or sub-deacons: see BCS. no. 442.
[2] Ib. no. 497.

Ceolnoth, however, was becoming an older man, and needed help with all this riding about. In 863 a grant of king Æthelred of Wessex was signed by him and three archdeacons of his familia;[1] another charter of the same period by the same three archdeacons and a fourth who had been promoted. Two other charters of 867 are signed by three or four archdeacons. Ceolnoth himself died in 870.

The need of delegating supervision, doing quasi-legal work, and seeing that canons passed by synods or in witans were obeyed in the parishes, remained. Since the duty of attending the king's witan was more constant for the two archbishops than the provincial bishops, they had indeed more instant need to delegate supervision. Supervision of the domestic affairs of their familia they could delegate, as other bishops did, to a *praepositus* or provost, later to a dean: supervision of their see must have been maintained largely, as before, by deacons. An archdeacon Agelnoth appears in a grant made by the archbishops Dunstan and Oscytel to Croyland in 966;[2] the see of Rochester had an archdeacon in 889, when Ciolmund, apparently of the Rochester familia, signed as archdeacon.[3] Ælfheah, archbishop from 1005 to 1012, apparently had an archdeacon Brinstan.[4]

Archbishop Ceolnoth, however, tried another experiment in devolution: the appointment of a 'chorepiscopus'. On the Continent the use of such a bishop, a country bishop 'without a see in a civitas', had been common in the eastern part of the Frankish lands, newly converted country, and, as having been outside the Roman empire, with few Germanic 'tuns' which could claim the status of a 'civitas'. The Frankish chorepiscopi had in fact been travelling bishops without see, in many cases, and were now regarded as irregular and undesirable. Ceolnoth, late in his episcopate, however, needed help in sacerdotal as well as administrative supervision, and such help a chorepiscopus could give; he therefore procured the appointment of the Christ Church presbyter Wighelm as, in modern terms, an assistant bishop. King Æthelred in 867, with the assent of archbishop Ceolnoth and his clergy, gave Wighelm 'a see in the place called the church of St. Martin and a small residence (villula) at that see, which rightly belongs to it.'[5]

Gervase of Canterbury, well read in the Canterbury archives,

---

[1] See Deanesly, M., 'The archdeacons of Canterbury under archbishop Ceolnoth', *supra*, p. 10-11.   [2] BCS. no. 1179.
[3] *Ib.* no. 562.   [4] ASW. 530.   [5] BCS. no. 516.

believed that the archbishop of Canterbury normally had a suffragan
bishop at St. Martin's, till that see was abolished by Lanfranc.
Eadsige, who became archbishop in 1038, was translated from St.
Martin's, and the ASC. states under the year 1044 that he resigned
from his archbishopric because of ill-health and consecrated Siward,
abbot of Abingdon, to be his suffragan there (whether expressly to
St. Martin's or not, we are not told): he did this with the counsel of
the king and earl Godwine, which suggests rather that Siward
was appointed coadjutor with expectation of the succession. In
1048, however, Siward resigned his bishopric because of ill-health
and archbishop Eadsige resumed his functions; Siward retired to
Abingdon but died that same year. Godwine appears as bishop of
St. Martin's in an annal of the ASC. for 1016, as dying in that year.[1]

It may be mentioned, with reference to the early importance of
the bishop's deacons, that there were many instances of abbots who
had been ordained deacons, but not priests, especially in the north
of England.[2] It was not strictly necessary that abbots should be in
clerical orders, but in the Celtic church all the monks had the
clerical tonsure and such clerical grades as they attained. It was not
infrequent before the ninth century that abbots should be deacons
only: in the gold and silver inscribed lists of benefactors and members
of the church of Durham (the *Liber Vitae Dunelmensis*[3]), one page is
devoted to columns of the names of abbots (of Lindisfarne and
Durham) who had attained the grade of priest (68 names) and
another page to the names of abbots of the grade of deacon, with
nine names; how far such monastic deacons had acquired notarial
technique, and with it administrative ability, is conjectural. There
are one or two cases of abbots not priests, however, from the south
of England.[4]

As to the see of York: there is good evidence of the existence of a
single archdeacon, an 'archidiaconus maior', but none of a plurality

---

[1] ASChar. no. 18. 'Godwine bishop at St. Martin's'.
[2] Cf. the number of abbot deacons quoted by Birch, in his *Fasti Monastici Aevi
Saxonici*, 1872.
[3] Facs. ed. in Surtees Soc. vol. 136 (1923), i. Many of the abbot deacons listed by
Birch in his *Fasti Monastici Aevi Saxonici*, 1872, are from the *Lib. Vit. Dunelm. Ecc.*
[4] See BCS. no. 539, where a grant of land in Kent originally made in 875 was
confirmed by archbishop Plegmund (890–914) and attested by 'Beornheah clericus
et abbas'.

11

of archdeacons. The *Northumbrian Priests' Law*,[1] which is concerned mainly with money penalties, lays down that the bot for disobedience to the bishop's edict is 20 oras, for disobedience to the archdeacon's, 10 oras. This implies that the archdeacon could issue mandates on his own authority: for if he had been acting merely in a secretarial capacity to the archbishop (as in issuing the summons to the diocesan synod), the bot would have been the archbishop's bot. The archdeacon would normally summon the rural priest for celebrating or otherwise acting irregularly.

As to the archdeacon's mandates or summonses, since the primary reason for creating archdeacons was the devolution of episcopal supervision, it is likely that they would have included warnings of the archdeacon's intention to visit a parish, and that he would there inquire along the lines stipulated by archbishop Hincmar of Reims for his archdeacons when making such a visit.[2] Hincmar had organised his large diocese more precisely than was the see of York: he had territorial archdeaconries: but the subjects of inquiry must have been similar, for the canons required the fulfilment of certain conditions in a parish. The archdeacons must beware of burdening the priests they visited by taking too large a train and requiring too much food for themselves and their horses; they must not accept or demand gifts from priests, or unite or divide rustic parishes on their own authority. They must ensure that no man have mass celebrated in his house without the bishop's leave, that no penitents are absolved for money, that they themselves do not present for ordination unsuitable candidates (rural priests who have themselves given some teaching to their young clerks might press the archdeacon to present them), that they ensure that priests maintain the church's property and a proper list of the poor to be fed (matricularii). Archbishop Hincmar himself laid down for his priests synodal rules that they must expound the creed and the Lord's Prayer every Sunday, administer the sacraments of baptism and penance, and maintain the altar, its furnishing, the altar vessels and the reserved sacrament whole, clean and shining, etc.; he required his archdeacons to see that his synodal rules were carried out. He did not specify money penalties for breaches of his laws: the fact that these are so prominent

---

[1] EHD. 434.
[2] See the commission sent to the archdeacons Guntarius and Odelhardus in 877: PL. 125, col. 799.

in the synodal rules of York indicates greater lawlessness there, and the difficulties of a half-converted Danish population.

A grant of king Edward the Confessor to Ealdred, archbishop of York, indicates that the work of an archdeacon was carried on with or without the title of archdeacon. To contemporaries indeed, such a phrase as 'the deacon of bishop so and so' implied that the subject was the man of business of the bishop's familia, without the special designation of 'archdeacon'. King Edward between 1060 and 1066 wrote to Leofric, bishop of Exeter,[1] informing him that he had granted the minster at Axminster (in the see of Exeter, but in the patronage of the kings of Wessex) to Ealdred, the deacon of archbishop Ealdred of York, 'as a pious benefaction to St. Peter's minster at York'. The minster would provide maintenance for an (arch)deacon's household, and would revert to the bishop's familia at York at his death.

Archdeacons and assistant bishops were an experiment in episcopal delegation, affecting a bishop's people in the city and the see at large. As his work increased however, a bishop was the less able to act as father to his community, monastic or canonical, in domestic matters, and here too delegation was necessary. Abbots with extensive estates and with private jurisdictions also needed assistance within the community; abbots must visit their estates at times, even though they had reeves in the villages; moreover, they attended 'synodal gemots' almost as frequently as bishops. Bishops and abbots needed a second self who should reside in the community, day in, day out, be responsible for the liturgical celebration of feasts and fasts, for discipline within the house, and for the training of the young clerks passing through the clerical orders, or the oblate children and novices, as the case might be.

St. Benedict in the sixty-fifth chapter of his rule had dealt with the question of a second in command under the abbot, a 'praepositus'. He had recommended that the abbot should, if possible, rule the monastery through deans (decani): delegated authority shared among many was less likely to lead to pride than when it was conferred only on one. Any association with 'ten' was long past when St. Benedict wrote of 'deans': to him they were intermediaries of no great importance, as in the Theodosian Code. Abbots like St. Benedict left their monasteries seldom: as is evidenced by the story

[1] ASW. 530.

in his Life, of how he visited his sister Scholastica, abbess of her own convent. She entreated him to stay the night, and he refused, saying he could by no means be absent from his monastery for a night. Then Scholastica put her head down on her hands and prayed to God, and a violent storm of rain came pouring down, which made it impossible for her brother to leave, much as he was aghast at the effect of his sister's prayer. To abbots who, like Benedict, very seldom left their houses, organisation through deans was possible; when frequent or even prolonged absences were necessary, delegation of authority to a single officer was unavoidable.

The term 'praepositus' was commonly used in Anglo-Saxon England for the second in command of minsters of all kinds: the term 'prior'[1] is only once found accompanying a witness's signature, and 'primus' (as first among the monks) only a few times.[2] After the Norman Conquest chroniclers, familiar with the 'priors' of Norman monasticism, might write of the pre-Conquest 'praepositi' as 'priors': but the Old English word for a monastic second was 'prafost', a 'mynster prafost'. (The word praepositus had a direct translation, gerêfa, reeve, as well as the borrowed, anglicised, Latin term prafost: but 'reeve' was used for the secular steward or bailiff, and prafost for an ecclesiastical deputy).

The Rule of Chrodegang was known in England in the ninth century and translated into English. Its chapter xliv, in the Old English version, is entitled 'About provosts' (Be tham prauostam) and runs:

> Though all who are superiors (the ealdordom habbath) in a community are rightly called 'praepositi', it is usual among us that those are called 'praepositi' who have a certain charge of priority (prioratus) under other prelates (ealdrum).

Chapter xlv goes on:

> It behoves the prelates of a church (mynstres ealdras) to choose from the congregation committed to them brothers of good repute with whom they may share the burden of government.[3]

The work 'prafost', praepositus, continued the normal term for the officer under bishop or abbot who attended to the internal affairs of

---

[1] See *infra* p. 159.
[2] For the 'primus' (monachorum) at Worcester, see *infra*, p. 163.
[3] See Napier, A. S., *The Old English version of the enlarged rule of Chrodegang together with the Latin original*, 1916, 52.

the house; a bishop who had a familia of monks or canons would have a prafost to share with him the burden of government of the house, and deacons, or a single archdeacon, (or in the case of ninth century Canterbury, three or four archdeacons), to share with him the burden or administration and supervision of the see. When the Benedictine reform and revival came with Æthelwold's work, however, it may be that 'praepositus' was too much associated with the internal affairs of the house to be quite appropriate for a monastic second officer who would have much to do with external affairs also: at any rate, it is from the time of Æthelwold that some Benedictine and canonical houses begin to be headed by a dean (decanus) under the abbot or bishop; a dean was an intermediary and the title did not, at the time, imply any independence of bishop or abbot.

The use of the title 'dean' in this late period of Old English church history rested on a knowledge of Roman law. The dean was an official go-between, a bearer of commands, as he had been in the Theodosian Code. On the Continent in the tenth century there was a 'rural dean' who was the senior of a local group of clergy, and the channel of communication between them and the bishop; similarly, the cathedral dean had a seniority among the canons and conveyed to them the bishop's paternal commands. The canons were still the bishop's cathedral familia; the dean as their senior was, to outsiders, the temporal and spiritual head of the community: but he held his office by virtue of his relation to the bishop. The tenth century saw the general feudalisation of society on the Continent, the grant of lay holdings in return for a specified amount of military service (the fief), and the gradual assimilation of other forms of land tenure to the fief. The early and pre-feudal deans, that is, were like the deans of Roman law, intermediaries: as now, the dean of a faculty of arts in a university is the intermediary between the professors and lecturers, and the vice-chancellor. The academic dean has no jurisdiction of his own over the members of the faculty: he could not judge them in his court and throw them into prison.

The peculiarity of the cathedral dean's position in France in the tenth century was that when society became feudalised, his position became feudalised also. The cathedral had a mensa, a landed estate and some cathedral lands owed military service. The dean's position came to be assimilated to that of a feudal landowner: he had a spiritual jurisdiction, originally the bishop's, over the large, cathedral parochia, and a spiritual jurisdiction over the clerks of the familia. But he had also the private, lay, jurisdiction over the courts on his estates and sometimes courts not on his church's estates: the profitable right of jurisdiction over such courts might have been bestowed upon his church as a benefaction. He would exercise it through a lay official (in England the reeve). His feudal position became of such importance that the sovereign, not the bishop, nominated him, and he took an oath of feudal loyalty to the sovereign. Only the sovereign could remove him, as he could remove any other feudal vassal for specified faults. The modern English cathedral dean continues, in fact, a tenth century, feudalised, dean, not merely a dean in Roman law. The cathedrals in England no longer have private courts for secular justice, nor do they owe the service of a specified number of knights; but the sovereign continues to appoint their deans, and they are irremovable, except by him. It is a very interesting survival of the feudal tenth century.

In England before the Norman Conquest, however, society was not yet feudalised in the Frankish manner. The bishop might owe a ship each summer to the king's sea forces, if his see included some great harbour, but he did not hold the lands of his see, or those of his cathedral familia, in return for the service of a specified number of knights;[1] nor did the dean of his familia. There is no definite evidence as yet to show that the sovereign, rather than the bishop, appointed the dean: neither the bishopric nor the deanery was as yet a fief of the crown. The dean was still the dean of Roman law: though the bishop's increasing absence from his cathedral city rendered the dean the more important.

Moreover, in the Confessor's reign, episcopal appointments were no longer made exclusively from the great monasteries; the king's writing officers, his chaplains who accompanied him and kept his relics, were increasingly appointed to sees. Such men, not trained as

---

[1] See, however, for the effect of king Edgar's endowment of the reformed monasteries with 'liberties' and 'privileges' as well as landed estates, Mr. Eric John's *Land tenure in early England*, 1960, especially his discussion of the Oswaldslow charters, pp. 80-126, which ends: 'The hundred looks very much indeed as though its well-known judicial and administrative functions must be set in a much more military context than hitherto'. It remains that the Oswaldslow charters, even at their face value, do not appear to confer land in return for the yearly service of a specified number of knights. The need of military defence, of course, operated in England as much as on the Continent: a final historical judgment as to the similarity of the means taken to supply it, in England and on the Continent, appears to have been not yet arrived at.

monks or canons, were the less likely to reside as long as possible with their cathedral clergy, monastic or secular, and the headship of the dean over the local church became the more independent and assured. For the year 1020, in Cnut's reign, the ASC. had written: 'On 13 November, Æthelnoth, a monk, who was dean at Christ Church, was consecrated bishop, with his see at Christ Church'; for 1033, 'Bishop Leofsige passed away (at Worcester) and Beorhtheah was raised to his see'; on the death of various bishops, only the names of their successors are given, and in some cases it appears they were from the cathedral monastery, monks or canons. But in 1043 the ASC. noted that 'Stigand the priest was consecrated bishop of East Anglia': he had worked in the royal scriptorium and was neither monk nor canon; in 1045, it was recorded that Beorhtwold (of Ramsbury) passed away and king Edward gave the bishopric to Herman, his chaplain; in 1047 bishop Grimcytel of Sussex passed away, and king Edward gave the bishopric to Heca, his chaplain; in 1049 Eadnoth, bishop of Oxfordshire, passed away, and Ulf, the priest (not a monk) was appointed as pastor of Eadnoth's bishopric, 'but later he was expelled, because he did nothing worthy of a bishop while he occupied the see'; in 1050 Eadsige, archbishop of Canterbury passed away, and 'the king gave the archbishopric to Robert the Frenchman', and in the same year he gave to bishop Rudolf, his kinsman, the abbacy of Abingdon; in 1052 'William the priest was given the bishopric of London'. Some monks were still made bishops: when bishop Wulfsige of Lichfield died in 1053, Leofwine, abbot of Coventry, succeeded to the bishopric, but with the increase of bishops who had been royal chaplains the office of dean gained importance.

The securest evidence about the officers through whom bishop or abbot managed their monks or their canons in the Old English church is the style following their names in the attestations to charters, and in the obituary lists of great monasteries. While important political decisions of the witan were attested by the king, members of the royal family, archbishops, bishops, abbots, dukes, ealdormen and thegns, local grants to a bishop or abbot, or leases of one or three lives, were often attested by the bishop, the abbot, the praepositus and the monks or clergy of the familia. These local grants speak of priest abbot or abbots (by this time an abbot was normally a priest), praepositi and deans: the term 'prior' is only once found, for a witness to a record of the synod of Clofesho, 825.[1] But the post-Conquest chroniclers were familiar with the term 'prior' for a monastic second officer, and they used it in their accounts of pre-Conquest history for officials who in their own day would have been called 'provost'. The term 'prior' in England in the eleventh century seems to have implied that, as first among the monks (either by election or seniority), he was not directly appointed by the abbot: the term was therefore suspect, or at any rate, unused.

The habit of post-Conquest historians of using the term 'prior' explains the frequent occurrence of 'prior' in such works as Dugdale's *Monasticon* and Birch's *Cartularium Saxonicum*. For instance, Dugdale gives a list of the 'priors' of Westminster, explaining that he means by 'priors', those who presided over the small, early community:[2] the names of the early priors he gives come from a charter now known to be spurious. For the Old Minster at Winchester Dugdale supplied a list of priors, or heads of the convent under the bishop,[3] but no pre-Conquest authority for the use of the term. For the monastery of Ely, he cites from the *Liber Eliensis*[4] a superior of the small monastery refounded after the destruction of the nunnery by the Danes: eight priests who had returned to the sacked minster had a superior, he says, termed the 'archipresbyter' or praepositus. Dugdale goes on to state that Brihtnoth, the 'prior' of Winchester, was appointed abbot when the monastery of Ely was refounded by Dunstan and Æthelwold. Many of Dugdale's instances of priors, again, are taken from the pseudo-Ingulph, whose history of Croyland, complete with forged charters, was actually composed by a Croyland monk in the fifteenth century.[5] Birch in many cases followed Dugdale and was not convinced that the pseudo-Ingulph's *Historia* was a spurious work.

[1] BCS. no. 385 from Cotton MS. Augustus ii. 78. This is a long, Latin form of the Old English no. 386, which has 'Torhthelm prio', according to Smith's *Beda*, p. 768, 'from a MS. in the possession of Lord Somers', not now available. See HS. iii. 605: and for the different forms of the *acta* of the synod of Clofesho, 824 and 825. Bede spoke of Ceolfrith as put in charge of Monkwearmouth, and of being at one time weary of the 'prioratus': Plummer notes that it is doubtful whether 'prioratus' was used technically for the office of prior: see Plummer, i, p. xxviii, n. 5. Nevertheless, Bede's expression renders a signature as 'prior' in 825 possible; though 'prior' does not occur in the Benedictine rule. (See p. 142). As to the prior Torhthelm who attested at Clofesho: he may have been the same as the Torhthelm who attested a royal grant of land in Kent to archbishop Wulfred in 814: see BCS. no. 348 and ASChar. no. 5.   [2] *Monast.* i. 267.   [3] *Ib.* i. 200.   [4] *Ib.* i. 458.
[5] See Gross, C., *The sources and literature of English history*, 1900, for the pseudo-Ingulph's *Historia Croylandensis*, no. 1371.

There are a few attestations by *praepositi*, before the tenth century reform, and only one instance of another name for a second officer occurs; the above mentioned 'prior' who attended the synod of Clofesho. When Ælfheah in 935 attested a grant of king Athelstan as 'Wintoniensis ecclesiae previsor',[1] it is unlikely that he meant the term 'provisor', which was sometimes used in monastic history as the equivalent of 'procurator'; it is more probable that he used it as a distinguished term for 'bishop': in another document he used 'speculator'.

As to the praepositus: three provosts, Athulgilsus, Ludhere and Dudda signed a record of the synod of Clofesho, 716.[2] At Canterbury, the minsters of Christ Church and St. Augustine's may have had provosts, as also in the early days may the familiae of Dover, Lyminge and Folkestone, considered as part of the archbishop's familia: the attestations to the synod of Aclea (Oakley), 844, are followed by a note: 'Here are the names of the familia of Christ (Church) and of that familia at Folkestone, and at Dover and at Lyminge who have sworn this oath, and their names are written beneath.'[3] Of these names, none are styled abbot or provost: they are only distinguished as priest or clerks not yet priests; the archbishop appears to have been reckoned head of the three minsters as well as Christ Church. A grant of the Mercian king, Kenulf, to St. Augustine's was attested by the provosts Wulfheard, Bearnhard and Eadred,[4] under the signature of archbishop Wulfred. The provosts Eanred and Biornhard attested a grant of archbishop Æthelheard in 805,[5] and Hæferth the provost a grant of archbishop Wulfred in 813.[6] A provost Aldberht signed next after abbot Ceolred of Medehamstede in 852 and was probably the provost of that house.[7]

In the see of Sherborne three provosts attested royal grants: when king Æthelberht of Wessex (860–866) granted an immunity to Sherborne, bishop Ahlstan (824–868) and Huita the provost attested;[8] there was no general gathering of prelates and, as the 23 other signatories were dukes and thegns and the king's relations, the three ecclesiastics, Ahlstan, Athhard the abbot and Huita the provost represented in some way the close interests of Sherborne. An abbot would

---

[1] BCS. no. 707.
[2] *Ib.* no. 91: of which the earliest source is a twelfth century copy of the record of a somewhat doubtful council.

[3] KCD. no. 256.	[4] BCS. no. 316.	[5] *Ib.* no. 319.
[6] *Ib.* no. 342.	[7] *Ib.* no. 464.	[8] ASChar. no. 11.

sign before a provost: one would expect that Huita was provost of Sherborne, though he may have been provost of some minster in the see temporarily without an abbot or whose abbot was not present. The royal grant was made at midwinter in 864, and a long note following it states that king Æthelberht on Good Friday laid the charter of freedom with his own hand upon the high altar (heah altare) of the monastery at Sherborne, in the presence of all the assembled brethren both old and young and of his two brothers, Æthelred and Alfred (the later king): and this was done in the presence of the witnesses recorded below. A long and slightly different list followed, and this time it included bishop Ahlstan's name and that of Torhthelm, 'deacon and provost', the only provost in the list. The very rare style, 'deacon and provost' suggests that here the minster of the provost was Sherborne, and that Torhthelm held the position of bishop's deacon as well as the headship of the familia under the bishop; the list includes this time the names of other members of the familia, six priests and two deacons. Huita does not sign; a later 'Huita the provost' attested a grant of king Edgar to Sherborne of between 960 and 975.

In the see of Wells, again, the office of provost continued throughout the pre-Conquest period. A record of the dues pertaining to Taunton 'on the day king Edward was alive and dead' (January 5, 1066) was attested by Giso, bishop of Wells, and 'Ælfnod mynster-pravost'.

On the whole, the number of attestations by provosts to charters is small: but though, in the case of an important grant, the provost of an episcopal minster might attest as well as the bishop of the church to which the grant was made, in other cases, when the officers of neighbouring minsters were called in to attest, the officer would be the abbot.

The use of the term 'praepositus' did not end with the tenth century reform, though some prelates began to appoint their second officers 'deans'. The matter is not dealt with specifically in the *Regularis Concordia*,' and though the work 'prior' occurs, it seems

---

[1] See *The Monastic Agreement of the Monks and Nuns of the English Nation* (edition and translation of the *Regularis Concordia*), by Dom Thomas Symons, 1953, p. xxx and n. The 'prior' is twice mentioned in a liturgical connexion, in the sense of abbot or senior monk in choir; the dean is directed to carry the serpent on the pole (before the abbot) on Good Friday (p. 39) and as a single officer under the abbot (p. 56). The praepositus appears as superior to the dean (p. 39).

there to mean the senior monk (in the sense of St. Benedict's rule) or the abbot himself.[1] Through the *Regularis Concordia*, which represented contemporary custom though directing it, any reformed house would be familiar with the praepositus, as second to the abbot according to the holy rule; with prior as a general word denoting abbot or the monk who took his place in chapel; and with the decanus as a single monastic officer, inferior to the provost but certainly having no connexion with 10 monks: the sense of dean in the Roman law books was by now generally accepted.

The circumstances leading to the appointment of a dean in a monastic house are perhaps best indicated in the case of the church at Worcester. Here the change of style for the officer heading the familia under the bishop appears to have been connected both with the introduction of monks to serve the episcopal see, and with the long absences, after 972, of bishop Oswald at York.

It was connected, first, with the planting of monks within the minster, and the building for them of the new church of St. Mary 'within the minster dedicated of old to St. Peter'. The supersession of the old community of clerks, headed by a provost, by a new monastic community headed by a 'primus (monachorum)' and then by a dean, appears certain from the anonymous Life of St. Oswald, and from the attestations to a long series of Worcester charters: the church at Worcester had a longer and more continuous series of charters than any other at the date.[1] The introduction of monks into the familia, and their amalgamation of such clerks of the old familia as chose to undertake the monastic life, is clear in general outline, but uncertain still in dating.

Charter evidence shows that the minster of St. Peter at Worcester before the Viking raids had a provost: Putta the provost attested a grant of bishop Ahlhun in 849,[2] and a provost attested a grant of 855, and another grant of bishop Wærferth in 872.[3] In 957 a grant of bishop Coenwald was attested by Behstan the priest, signing next after the bishop, without special title, and by the priests, deacons and clerks of the familia.[4] In 899 another grant of this bishop was attested

---

[1] See Robinson, J. Armitage, *St. Oswald and the church of Worcester*, Brit. Acad. Supp. Papers no. v (1919), for a detailed discussion of the various Worcester charters; and Mr. Eric John in *St. Oswald*, bibliog., p. 174.

[2] BCS. no. 455.

[3] *Ib.* no. 533. (Æthelhard the provost).   [4] *Ib.* no. 992.

by Cynelm, 'abbot and deacon': he signed next after the bishop as the head, apparently, of the familia at Worcester.[1]

Oswald became bishop in 961, and received the contingent of Ramsey monks hardly before 968–969: but it does not follow that he had done nothing to prepare for the 'monachization' of his familia before that. The process is difficult to trace from the attestations to the Worcester charters: for most monks now became priests, moved up through the clerical grades, and might as readily be styled 'deacon', 'priest' or 'clerk' after their attestation, as by the comprehensive term 'monachus'. 'Clericus' implied that a man had the tonsure and was not a layman; but a monk also had the tonsure and was not a layman: he might be described as 'clericus' if he were neither deacon nor priest; in contemporary witness lists it was usual to distinguish priests and deacons, and to classify the holders of minor orders generally as 'clerici'. A land grant or lease was a legal document, and, remembering the different values as oath helper or warrantor attached to the status of priest, deacon, cleric or layman, it is natural that the clerical grades should be used in attestations more frequently than the term 'monk': they assess the importance of the signatory as a witness. There is no proof that in Oswald's later grants, after 968–969, when the witnesses, after the bishop, were graded as priests, deacons and clerks, that they were not monks. It is even likely that they were.

As to the monk in charge of the community under Oswald: in 965 he granted land for three lives, with the consent and leave 'of all those of monastic conversation', i.e. of the community of St. Mary in the monastery 'whose episcopal chair is dedicated to St. Peter', to 'Athelstan primus', whose subscription followed his own and was followed by those of three priests, three deacons and some clerks.[2] Athelstan was certainly a priest,[3] and the style 'primus' can be nothing but 'primus monachorum' or 'primus claustri'.[4] He

---

[1] BCS. no. 580; see *supra*.

[2] *Ib.* no. 1166. In no. 1167 another form of the lease, Athelstan also attests as 'primus'.

[3] He had attested a grant of Oswald to his 'artifex Wulfhelm' as 'Athelstan the priest', and he similarly attested Oswald's grant to the thegn Eadmær in 967: BCS. nos. 1184 and 1203.

[4] Mr. Eric John, *supra, St. Oswald*, 164, discusses whether the signatories to Oswald's charters were all members of his familia, and refers to a grant to a clericus who was possibly a monk as 'odd'. The 'primus', or later the dean, would have, however, to supervise monastic lands and even franchises; he would need a few horses and servants: he would need a 'household'.

would be responsible for the liturgical observance and the domestic routine of the house: bishop Oswald would still, as the *Regularis Concordia* directs, live with the community and be its abbot.

The next step was the reception of a contingent of trained monks from Ramsey, under the leadership of Wynsige the monk. Two Latin grants of Oswald, copied into Hemming's cartulary, have brief Anglo-Saxon notes at their ends mentioning Wynsige: the notes would seem to have been added early, in place of a witness list. The first is a grant dated 969 to Oswald's trusted Byrnric, to hold for his life and bequeath to two other clerks for life, the land returning then to the church of Worcester; the scribe added, at some time later than 969 (but before Wynsige was dean) the words:

> This was done by the witness of Wynsige the monk and all the monks of Worcester.[1]

The second Anglo-Saxon note is attached to a lease granted by Oswald in 974:

> This was done by the witness of Wynsige the dean and all the monks at Worcester.[2]

The change of style for the head of the community under Oswald from 'primus' to 'decanus' (we do not know that it was made immediately on the arrival of Wynsige: though, as the Ramsey monk who wrote St. Oswald's life says he had been 'our dean', it is likely) must have been of importance when, in 972, Oswald was made archbishop. In monastic tradition, a dean was a third officer under provost and abbot and concerned with the domestic affairs of the house; in notarial language on the other hand, a dean was a messenger and an intermediary, but his message carried the full authority of the sender. Wynsige was now not merely the first of the monks: he spoke with the authority of the archbishop-bishop to all the seculars and ecclesiastics in the see of Worcester. After his promotion as dean, the office of 'primus' of the monks, in charge of the domestic affairs of the house, was apparently maintained: 'Winsinus primus' (i.e. Wynsige) attested a grant of Oswald's in 982, and Athelstan, who had once been primus, attested simply as presbyter.[3] The deanery of the monastic house of Worcester was also maintained, for a grant

---

[1] BCS. no. 1243.   [2] *Ib.* no. 1298.
[3] Cotton MS. Tiberius A. xiii, f. 113; KCD. no. 624.

of king Edward was attested by Æthelwinus, 'the dean of the church at Worcester', and the same Æthelwinus the dean attested a charter of bishop Lyfing of Worcester in 1052–1053.[1]

As to Christ Church, Canterbury, there is no very early attestation by a dean: presumably, till archbishop Ælfric (995–1005) made the house fully Benedictine, the archbishops used their deacons as their official deputies, or the provost of the minster. Archbishop Æthelnoth, surnamed 'the Good', was, however, dean of Christ Church before he was consecrated archbishop in 1020.[2] Godric, the dean of Christ Church, attested many documents: in 1044 he attested one between archbishop Eadsige and Æthelric in company with all the familia (hired) at Christ Church:[3] another of the years between 1044 and 1048, under the names of Eadsige and Siward his coadjutor, and another, a grant of Eadsige to St. Augustine's abbey.[4]

There is more evidence about the deans of the New Minster at Winchester (Hyde Abbey), because we possess in Stowe MS. 944 the *Liber Vitae* of the abbey.[5] To this illuminated altar book with the gospels for certain great feasts and Sundays were added the forms for some liturgical ceremonies, certain charters, and the *Liber Vitae* itself: the lists of founders, benefactors, bishops and abbots closely connected with the abbey, the list of the abbots, officers and members of the community, and the lists of those who had commended themselves to the prayers of the brethren or who had a special devotion to the abbey. The lists were carried on into the post-Conquest period: but the Anglo-Saxon names can be distinguished from the Norman. In the list of the community members, where every name is followed by a descriptive word (abbot, priest, deacon, conversus), many oblate boys must have died young (strings of names in succession suggest, as in an epidemic) for they are described simply as 'puer'.

Among the members of the Hyde community appears the name

---

[1] KCD. no. 807; ASWills, 457.

[2] ASW. p. 554. The ASC. has, under the year 1020, 'Archbishop Lyfing passed away, and Æthelnoth, monk and dean at Christ Church, was consecrated bishop thereto in that same year.'

[3] ASChar. no. 101.   [4] *Ib.* nos. 103, 108.

[5] Printed by Birch, W. de G., in the Hants. Rec. Soc. 1892. Other communities kept records of members and benefactors like the New Minster *Liber Vitae*: the most famous surviving MS. is the *Liber Vitae Dunelmensis* (see p. 153); here, however, the pre-Conquest entries, though arranged in categories, have no descriptive terms. B.M. Addit. MS. 40.000, the obit list of Thorney abbey, Cambs., has few pre-Conquest entries, and no reference to dean or provost.

of Ælfric the dean (of the New Minster), whose name occurs in that curious twelfth century compilation, the letter of Edwin the monk to bishop Ælfsige,[1] which speaks also of Leofwine, a dean of the Old Minster. Another dean of the New Minster, Wihtsige, also appears in the *Liber Vitae*. The deans mentioned can have attained no higher rank: any dean who was promoted abbot would have appeared in the *Liber Vitae* under that style.

Among the lists of those with a special devotion to the New Minster (and therefore not members of the community) appear Godwine II, the dean, and 'Godefridus prior': but the latter appears late in the list and was probably Norman. 'Leofwine, monk and dean' appears; and 'Ælfweard, dean and priest' appears soon after in the list, and, nine names later, 'Ælfric the provost and priest': which may suggest that Ælfweard was third, not second in command under the abbot at the time.

There is evidence, again, for a dean at the minster of Bury St. Edmunds: an agreement of between 1051 and 1065 was attested by 'Stigand the bishop, Ufi the abbot and Leofstan the dean' (of Bury St. Edmunds).[2] Ufi the abbot had been provost of St. Benedict's, Hulme[3] till he was made abbot of Bury in 1020, and Leofstan the dean became abbot of Bury.[4] The occurrence of a provost of Hulme and a dean of Bury in the same document inspires a query whether monasteries still, as in the *Regularis Concordia* could be organised with both provost and dean under the abbot: but this document is some 80 years later than the *Regularis Concordia*, and it is certain that Leofstan the dean headed the community under the abbot, as when 'Leofstan the dean and all the community of Bury St. Edmunds' attested the will of Thurstan among the Suffolk witnesses.[5]

The minster of Evesham also had a dean: the ASC., under the year 1037, speaks of the banishment of the Lady Ælfgifu-Emma, to Flanders: 'and earlier in the year Æsic, the noble dean of Evesham, passed away'. Monasteries of monks were now headed by deans, under abbot or bishop, as often as monasteries of canons.

Hazarding a guess where evidence is incomplete: the more old-fashioned communities, in the half century before the Norman Conquest, had provosts: the larger, better informed, and perhaps

---

[1] See ASW. no. 113 and notes.
[2] ASChar. no. xcvii.   [3] See *ib.* p. 445.
[4] *Ib.* no. 103; ASWills, no. 26. This will is that of bishop Ælfric of Elmham or East Anglia: probably Ælfric II, 1023-1039.   [5] ASWills, no. xxxi.

more closely in touch with the Continent, had deans. The early provosts of the northern minsters, Beverley and Ripon, were the normal pre-Conquest minster provosts: their position and powers changed after the Conquest. The small communities in the south of England: the minsters of the west, and the minsters of the north except for the archiepiscopal house at York, had provosts; while the great communities of the south, Christ Church, the Old and New Minsters at Winchester, Worcester, Bury and Evesham, used for their head under a superior the newer title of dean, with its implication in notarial usage.

The growing prosperity of the minsters in the late Old English period is reflected in a certain specialisation of function. Not only does the more complex administrative work of bishop and abbot give greater importance to the work of archdeacons (or deacons) and deans, but the community of monks or clerics becomes increasingly separated from their abbot and bishop in daily life. The monk-bishop has obvious spiritual duties which take him abroad in the diocese; but abbots and bishops alike owe attendance at times on the king's court, are responsible for the running of landed estates by their reeves and sometimes for the doing of justice in the hundred moot. Both have to exercise considerable hospitality to travellers of all ranks: sometimes to the king. Their daily life and meal times cannot always accord with the monastic time-table: both superiors need a small household of servants and horses. The maintenance of the community, its food and clothing, is only one item to be met from the abbot or bishop's revenue. The apportionment of revenue cannot as yet be provided for by allocating a fraction of a money revenue to different needs, for addition and subtraction by the use of Roman numerals on parchment is almost impossible, and the revenue itself will be received partly in kind. While the offerings in church will be received in silver pennies, and the fixed rent (feorm) of some few abbey lands may be in pounds of silver pennies, by weight, the feorm of other estates will be received in corn or malt or provender of some kind. Tithe may be received in sheaves, or a payment arrived at by bargaining instead. Many benefactions of individuals by will had included the payment, once or twice a year, of a specified food offering to a minster, for the soul of the bene-factor. Revenue was miscellaneous.

The evidence of wills shows that by this time the familia, the 'hird' of all the large minsters had an endowment separate from the total revenue of abbot or bishop, which had sufficed earlier both for the superior of the minster and the hird. It was one way of dealing with the difficulty of accounting, and also it secured the maintenance of the hird while the headship of the minster was vacant and the estates in the king's (or some lay patron's) hands. No complaints are met with at the time of the deliberate keeping of abbacies and bishoprics vacant, for Cnut and Edward the Confessor cherished the monks as the earlier tenth century kings had done; but on the Continent this was a powerful motive for giving the 'hird' a separate revenue.

The community at Christ Church, Canterbury, had long had a separate endowment, and it continued to receive food allowances, and estates, from various benefactors. Æthelwyrd, a Kentish land-owner, before 958 left the reversion of an estate to the community, to receive from the interim holder, Eadric, in his life time, a gift of five pounds (two to the senior members, and three to the whole community) and an annual rendering to the 'hird' at Michaelmas of 40 sesters of ale, 60 loaves, a wether sheep, a flitch of bacon and an ox's haunch, together with two cheeses, four hens and five pence.[1] Many wills at the time specify food renderings in similar detail. Between 975 and 991 the lady Ælflæd, the second wife of king Edmund, bequeathed an estate to the 'hird' of Christ Church, and also two estates to St. Paul's minster in London, one for the bishop's use and one for the 'hird' there.[2] Æthelric similarly bequeathed an estate to the hird of Christ Church, and another to St. Paul's minster in London, 'for lights' and 'to deal Christendom to God's folk', i.e. for the bishop and his pastoral work.[3]

The king's chaplains received estates as salary, and a writ of king Cnut and his queen attributed to the year 1032 permitted their priest Eadsige to dispose of the Kentish estate they had given him as he wished. He became a monk at Christ Church, and gave the estate to the hird there, 'buying it back for his own life time and Edwin's for 4 pounds: on condition that every year 3 weys of cheese and 3 binds of eels should be rendered to Christ Church from the estate'; this wealthy chaplain also bought from the hird for his life time and Edwin's another estate for 4 pounds, both estates to pass to the hird

[1] ASChar. no. 32.　　　[2] ASWills, no. 15.　　　[3] Ib. no. 16 (1).

12

at his death. Not only that, but he bought an estate at Orpington for 80 marks of white silver by the standard of the husting (a very large price) 'to provide clothing for the servants of God': and he granted two other estates after his and Edwin's death 'to provide food for the servants of God'. The continued holding by a Bene-dictine monk of considerable estates may have arisen from his joint holding of them with Edwin: but it is notable that the hird at Christ Church now had an endowment for their refectory separate from the endowment of their wardrobe.[1] Another gift towards the 'food and clothing' of the hird at Christ Church occurs in an agree-ment made by archbishop Eadsige in 1044.[2] A grant by Thurstan to the refectory at Christ Church is accompanied by the stipulation that the Christ Church hird shall pay from the endowment 12 pounds a year to the hird of St. Augustine's.[3] The will of Wulfgyth, of 1046, made a grant to 'foster' (i.e. feed) the monks of the hird at Christ Church.[4]

Among the minsters of monks and canons which had endowments for the hird, and sometimes separate endowments for refectory and wardrobe, the following grants are mentioned in wills. The lady Æthelflæd, between 1004 and 1014, bequeathed an estate to St. Paul's minster in London 'for the maintenance of the brethren who daily serve God there'.[5] The endowment of the 'lord of the church' at Medehamstede had been separate from that of the refectory of the community as early as 852.[6] The property of Ramsey abbey was divided between abbot and community: the wealthy thegn, Ælfhelm, bequeathed between 975 and 1016 'my long ship to Ramsey, half for the abbot and half for the community'.[7] Wulfrid Spott, the son of the Wulfrun who endowed a church of canons at Wolver-hampton, and who was the founder or refounder of the minster of Burton-on-Trent, in his will of 1002–1004 bequeathed an estate to the 'hired' at Tamworth, and many estates to the 'monks' at Burton, including the land on which the minster stood.[8] King Athelstan in 934 granted three estates to the hird of the Old Minster at Winchester, for their food and clothing (beodlandæ and hregl-talæ).[9]

[1] ASChar. no. 86.   [2] Ib. no. 101.   [3] ASWills, nos. 30 and 31.
[4] Ib. no. 32.   [5] Ib. no. 22.   [6] ASChar. no. 7.
[7] ASWills, no. 13.   [8] Ib. no. 17.   [9] ASChar. no. 25.

BIBLIOGRAPHICAL NOTE

FOR reference to the background of these studies in pre-Conquest church history the two relevant volumes in the Oxford History of England are most useful: Collingwood, R. G. and Myres, J. N. L., *Roman Britain and the English Settlements*, 1936; Stenton, F. M., *Anglo-Saxon England*, 1943 and 1947.

For an extremely valuable discussion of sources and bibliography, together with selected translations of the more important sources, narrative and documentary, see Professor Dorothy Whitelock's section in Part iii of her *English Historical Documents*, pp. 567-854; and for an exhaustive bibliography which lists under subjects both books and the relevant articles in periodicals: Bonser, W., *An Anglo-Saxon and Celtic Bibliography (450-1087)*, 2 vols., 1957.

CONTRACTIONS

ASC. *Anglo-Saxon Chronicle*: the Everyman's Library ed., no. 624, ed. by G. N. Garmonsway; for text, Plummer, C., *Two of the Saxon Chronicles parallel*, 1892–1899.

ASChar. Robertson, A. J., *Anglo-Saxon Charters*, 1939.

ASW. Harmer, F. E., *Anglo-Saxon Writs*, 1952.

ASWills. Whitelock, D., *Anglo-Saxon Wills*, 1930.

BCS. Birch, W. de G., *Cartularium Saxonicum*, 4 vols. 1885–1889.

BHL. *Bibliotheca Hagiographica Latina*, ed. Soc. Bollandiani, 2 vols. 1898–1901, with suppl. 1911. (For saints of whom there is a written Life: for Celtic saints, of whom there is often no Life, see Gould, S. Baring and J. Fisher, *Lives of the British Saints*, 4 vols., published by the Cymmrodorion Soc. (Supplementary vols.), 1907-13.)

Darlington. 'Ecclesiastical Reform in the late Old English period', in EHR. li (1936).

EBC. *Studies in the Early British Church*, ed. Chadwick, Nora K., 1958.

EHD. *English Historical Documents*, c. 500–1042, ed. Whitelock, D., 1955.

EHR. *The English Historical Review*.

Ellard. Ellard, G., *Ordination Anointings in the Western Church before 1000 A.D.*, Med. Acad. of America, Publications no. 16, 1933.

HE. Bede's *Historia Ecclesiastica Gentis Anglorum*; for Latin text and notes, see ed. of Plummer, C., 2 vols., 1896; for English translation, the Everyman ed., no. 479, with introd. by Prof. David Knowles.

HS. Haddan, A. W. and Stubbs, W., *Councils and ecclesiastical documents relating to Great Britain and Ireland*, 3 vols., 1869–1871.

JEH. *Journal of Ecclesiastical History*.

KCD. Kemble, J. M., *Codex Diplomaticus Anglo-Saxonicus*, 6 vols., 1839–1848.

MGH. *Monumenta Germaniae Historica*.

MOE. *The Monastic Order in England*, Knowles, Dom David, 1940.

Monast. Dugdale, W., *Monasticon Anglicanum*, 6 vols., 1846 *seqq.*

PL. *Patrologia Latina*, ed. the abbé J.-P. Migne.

Plummer. *Venerabilis Baedae* (*historia ecclesiastica*), ed. C. Plummer, 2 vols., 1896.

Rice. *English Art 871–1100*, Rice, D. Talbot, 1952.

BIBLIOGRAPHY

Acta Sanctorum, ed. Johannes Bollandus, 1643 *seqq.*

Anderson, A. O. 'Ninian and the southern Picts', in *Scottish Historical Review*, xxvii (1948), 25.

Ashdown, M. *English and Norse documents*, 1930. (See for some references to barbaric cruelty of the Northmen.)

Bethurum, D. *The homilies of Wulfstan*, 1957. See for text and introduction.

Blair, P. H. *An introduction to Anglo-Saxon England*, 1959, for much information about the later Anglo-Saxon church, diocesan boundaries, etc.

Brown, G. Baldwin. *The arts in early England*, 6 vols. (in 7), 1903–1937; *From schola to cathedral*, 1886.

Bruce-Mitford, R. L. S. ed. *Recent Archaeological Excavations in Britain*, 1956, for articles on Mithraic remains at Carrawburgh and on the Walbrook and on Lullingstone; *The Sutton Hoo Ship-Burial*, 1949.

Chadwick, N. K. *Studies in early British history*, 1954, specially for the Bernicians, and early dedications in the Welsh church; 'St. Ninian', in *Trans. of the Dumfriesshire and Galloway Nat. Hist. and Antiq. Soc.*, vol. xxvii.

Chavasse, A. *Le Sacramentaire gélasien (Vaticanus Reginensis 316): sacramentaire presbytéral en usage dans les titres romains au VIIᵉ siècle*, 1958.

Clapham, A. W. *English Romanesque Architecture before the Norman Conquest*, 1930.

Clemoes, P. *The Anglo-Saxons: studies presented to Bruce Dickins*, 1959, specially for pre-Conquest churches.

Crawford, S. J. *The Old English version of the Heptateuch, Ælfric's treatise on the Old and New Testament and his Preface to Genesis*, E.E.T.S. O.S.160, 1922; *Byrhtferth's Manual*, vol. i, 1929.

Cruden, S. *The early Christian and Pictish Monuments of Scotland*, 1957: for the Whithorn stones.

Darlington, R. R. *The Vita Wulfstani*, Camden Soc. 3rd Ser., 1928; 'The Anglo-Saxon Period', in *The English Church and the Continent*, ed. Dodwell, C. R., 1959.

Davis, G. R. C. *Medieval Cartularies*, 1958; useful for charter material.

Deanesly, M. 'The Canterbury Edition of the Answers of pope Gregory I to St. Augustine', in JEH. x (1959), 1-49; 'The archdeacons of Canterbury under archbishop Ceolnoth', EHR. xlii (1927), 1-11.

Dix, G. *The shape of the liturgy*, 1943, and for more recent work on the evolution of the liturgy, Baumstark, A., *Comparative Liturgy*, English ed. of F. L. Cross, 1953.

Doble, G. H. *The Lanalet Pontifical*, 1934; see for the 'Pontifical of Egbert', Surtees Soc., 1853; and many short tracts on Celtic saints.

Duckett, E. S. *Saint Dunstan of Canterbury*, 1955.

Ekwall, E. *The concise dictionary of English place names*, 4th ed. 1960; and for place names also, Mawer, A. and Stenton, F. M. *Introduction to the survey of English place names*, 1924.

Evans, A. W. Wade-. *Welsh Christian Origins*, 1934; *Vitae Sanctorum Britanniae Genealogiae* (with trans.), 1944; *The Emergence of England and Wales*, 1959: valuable, but controversial in parts.

Förster, M. *Zur Geschichte des Reliquienskultus in Altengland*, Sitzungsberichte der Bayerischen Akad. der Wissenschaften, Heft 8, 1943.

Gildas. *De excidio et conquestu Britanniae*: Eng. trans., see Giles, J. A., *Gildas and Nennius*, 1842–1845; and also in Wade-Evans, A. W., *Nennius' Hist. of the Britons*, 1938, 122–153.

Gould, S. Baring. *The Lives of the Saints*, 16 vols., 1897, 98.

Grosjean, P. 'Confusa Caligo', in Zeuss memorial vol. published by *Celtica*, Dublin, 1955, for the Hisperica Famina and the inflated Latin in the period between Aldhelm and 1066; 'Notes d'hagiographie celtique' in the *Analecta Bollandiana*, lxxv (1957), 158-226, for St. Patrick and his stay at Auxerre under Germanus; *ib.* lxxviii (1960), 'La Date du Colloque de Whitby'.

John, E. 'St. Oswald and the tenth century reformation', in JEH. ix (1958), 159–172; 'An alleged Worcester charter in the reign of Edgar', in the *Bull. of the John Rylands Library*, 1958; 'The king and the monks in the tenth century reformation', *ib.* 1959; 'Some Latin charters of the tenth century reformation in England, in *Revue Bénédictine*, lxx (1960), 333-359; *Land tenure in early England*, 1960.

Kemp, E. W. *Canonization and authority in the Western Church*, 1948.

Kendrick, T. D. *Anglo-Saxon Art to A.D. 900*, 1938; *Late Saxon and Viking Art*, 1949.

Ker, N. R. *Catalogue of manuscripts containing Anglo-Saxon*, 1957.

Liebermann, F. *Die Gesetze der Angelsachsen*, 3 vol. 1898–1916.

Lloyd, J. E. *History of Wales to the Edwardian Conquest*, 3rd ed. 1939: for early Welsh saints.

Lowe, E. A. *The Bobbio Missal: a Gallican mass-book, M.S. Paris 13246*.

Malmesbury, William of, *De antiquitate Glastoniensis Ecclesiae*, in Adam of Domerham's ed., 1727.

Meates, G. W. *Lullingstone Roman villa*, 1955: also Reports in 'Archaeologia Cantiana', lxiii (1951) and lxv (1953).

Mortimer, R. C. *Western Canon Law*, 1953.

Oleson, T. J. *The Witenagemot in the reign of Edward the Confessor*, 1955.

Plucknett, T. F. T. *A concise history of common law*.

Powicke, Sir F. M. and Fryde, E.B. *Handbook of British Chronology*, 1961 (for bishops).

Raby, F. J. E. *A history of Christian Latin poetry, from the beginnings to the close of the middle ages*, 1953.

Renwick, W. S. and Orton, H. *The beginnings of English literature*, vol. i, 1952. See for manuscript sources, etc.

Rice, D. Talbot. *The beginnings of Christian Art*, 1957.

Richmond, I. A. *Roman and Native in North Britain*, 1958.

Robertson, A. J. *The Laws of the kings of England from Edmund to Henry I*, 1925.

Robinson, J. A. *St. Oswald and the church of Worcester*, 1919; *The Saxon bishops of Wells*, 1918; *Somerset historical essays*, 1921; *The times of St. Dunstan*, 1922.

Saxl, F. *Memorial Essays*, 1957, for 'Implications of the term *Sapiens* as applied to Gildas', Deanesly, M.

Schramm, P. E. *History of the English Coronation*, 1937.

Simpson, W. D. *The Celtic church in Scotland*, 1935.

Stenton, F. M. *The early history of the abbey of Abingdon*, 1913; 'The South-Western element in the Old English Chronicle', in *Essays presented to Thomas Frederick Tout*, 1925; *The Latin Charters of the Anglo-Saxon period*, 1954; Introduction to the Phaidon ed. of *The Bayeux Tapestry*, 1957.

Stevenson, J. *The historical works of Simeon of Durham*, trans., 1855: useful for northern church history.

Stutz, U. 'The proprietary church as an element of medieval Germanic ecclesiastical law', in *Medieval Germany, 911–1250*, vol. ii of *Essays by German historians*, trans. G. Barraclough, 1938.

Sweet, H. *Selected Homilies of Ælfric*, 1922.

Symons, T. *The Monastic Agreement of the monks and nuns of the English nation* (Regularis Concordia), 1953.

Thompson, A. Hamilton. 'Diocesan Organization in the Middle Ages: Archdeacons and Rural Deans', 1943. *Proc. of the Brit. Academy*, xxiv; *Liber Vitae Ecclesiae Dunelmensis*, Surtees Soc. vol. 136, 1923.

Thompson, E. A. 'The origin of Christianity in Scotland', in *Scottish Historical Review*, xxxvii (1958), 17-22.

Thorpe, B. *Ancient laws and institutes of England*, 1840; *Homilies of Ælfric*, 2 vols. 1843–1846.

Toynbee, J. M. C. 'Christianity in Roman Britain', *Jour. of the Brit. Archaeol. Assoc.*, 3rd S., xvi (1953), covers all the archaeological evidence.

Victoria County History. Each county has an early volume with a section dealing with ecclesiastical and monastic history.

Wainwright, F. T. *The problem of the Picts*, 1955.

Wardale, E. E. *Chapters on Old English Literature*, 1935.

Watkin, Dom Aelred. *The Great Chartulary of Glastonbury*, 1947 *seqq.*

White, Caroline L. *Aelfric: a new study of his life and writings*, 1898: Yale Studies in English, ii.

Whitelock, D. *Sermo Lupi ad Anglos*, 1939; *The audience of Beowulf*, 1951; *The beginnings of English society*, 1952; *English historical documents*, vol. i, 1955.

Wilson, H. A. *The Gelasian Sacramentary*, 1893.

Wilkins, D. *Concilia Magnae Britanniae et Hiberniae*, 4 vols., 1737.

INDEX